SAVING ENDANGERED SPECIES

THE BIGHORN SHEEP

Help Save This Endangered Species!

Stephen Feinstein

MyReportLinks.com Books

an imprint of

Enslow Publishers, Inc.

Box 398, 40 Industrial Road
Berkeley Heights, NJ 07922
USA

MyReportLinks.com Books, an imprint of Enslow Publishers, Inc. MyReportLinks®
is a registered trademark of Enslow Publishers, Inc.

Library of Congress Cataloging-in-Publication Data

Feinstein, Stephen.
  The bighorn sheep : help save this endangered species! / Stephen Feinstein.
    p. cm. — (Saving endangered species)
  Includes bibliographical references and index.
  ISBN-13: 978-1-59845-042-2
  ISBN-10: 1-59845-042-5
  1. Bighorn sheep—Juvenile literature. I. Title.
QL737.U53F45 2008
599.649'7—dc22
                                    2006028916

Printed in the United States of America

10 9 8 7 6 5 4 3 2 1

To Our Readers:
Through the purchase of this book, you and your library gain access to the Report Links that specifically
back up this book.

The Publisher will provide access to the Report Links that back up this book and will keep these Report
Links up to date on **www.myreportlinks.com** for five years from the book's first publication date.

We have done our best to make sure all Internet addresses in this book were active and appropriate when
we went to press. However, the author and the Publisher have no control over, and assume no liability
for, the material available on those Internet sites or on other Web sites they may link to.

The usage of the MyReportLinks.com Books Web site is subject to the terms and conditions stated on the
Usage Policy Statement on **www.myreportlinks.com**.

A password may be required to access the Report Links that back up this book. The password is found
on the bottom of page 4 of this book.

Any comments or suggestions can be sent by e-mail to comments@myreportlinks.com or to the address
on the back cover.

Photo Credits: © Corel Corporation, pp. 3, 16, 27, 51, 53, 64–65, 68–69, 95, 114–115; © Larsek/
Shutterstock.com, pp. 1, 11; © Shutterstock.com, pp. 37, 40, 46–47, 49, 59, 66, 71, 75, 78, 103;
© Ronnie Howard/Shutterstock.com, p. 25; Columbia Basin Fish and Wildlife Compensation Program,
p. 110; Enslow Publishers, Inc., p. 5; Foundation for North American Wild Sheep, p. 26; Government of
Yukon, p. 32; Hells Canyon National Recreation Area, p. 82; Hinterland Who's Who, p. 44; Library of
Congress, pp. 10, 91, 93, 97; Montana Fish, Wildlife and Parks Department, p. 72; MyReportLinks.com
Books, p. 4; National Geographic.com, p. 34; National Park Service, pp. 12, 81, 90; NatureServe, p. 77;
New Hampshire Public Television, p. 61; Petroglyphs.US, p. 84; San Diego Zoo, p. 111; The Arizona
Game and Fish Department, p. 108; The Arizona-Sonora Desert Museum, p. 55; The Bighorn Institute,
p. 30; The Colorado Division of Wildlife, p. 88; The Desert Bighorn Council, p. 57; The Living Desert Zoo
and Gardens, p. 14; The Sierra Nevada Bighorn Sheep Foundation, p. 24; The Texas Bighorn Society,
p. 113; The Utah Division of Wildlife Resources, p. 101; The Yosemite Association, p. 99; U.S. Fish and
Wildlife Service, pp. 20, 36, 105, 106, 117; United States House of Representatives, p. 22; University of
California, Berkeley, p. 18; University of Michigan Museum of Zoology, p. 42; William S. Myerson Photo
Imagery, p. 86.

Cover Photo: Bighorn sheep, Rocky Mountain National Park, © Larsek/Shutterstock.com.

CONTENTS

MyReportLinks.com Books
Great Books, Great Links, Great for Research!

The Internet sites featured in this book can save you hours of research time. These Internet sites—we call them **"Report Links"**—are constantly changing, but we keep them up to date on our Web site.

When you see this "Approved Web Site" logo, you will know that we are directing you to a great Internet site that will help you with your research.

Give it a try! Type http://www.myreportlinks.com into your browser, click on the series title and enter the password, then click on the book title, and scroll down to the Report Links listed for this book.

The Report Links will bring you to great source documents, photographs, and illustrations. MyReportLinks.com Books save you time, feature Report Links that are kept up to date, and make report writing easier than ever! A complete listing of the Report Links can be found on pages 118–119 at the back of the book.

Please see "To Our Readers" on the copyright page for important information about this book, the MyReportLinks.com Web site, and the Report Links that back up this book.

Please enter **BHS1583** if asked for a password.

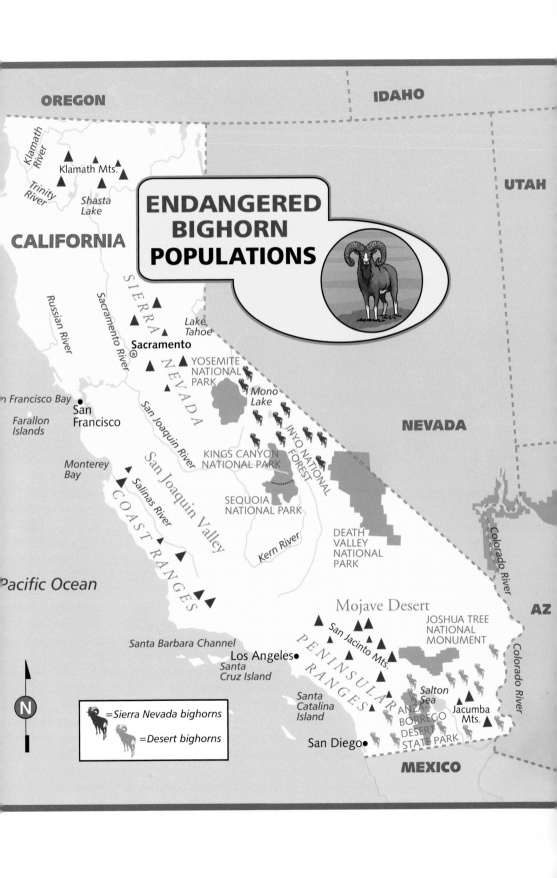

OREGON

IDAHO

UTAH

CALIFORNIA

Klamath Mts.

Klamath River

Trinity River

Shasta Lake

ENDANGERED BIGHORN POPULATIONS

SIERRA NEVADA

Lake Tahoe

Sacramento River

Sacramento

Russian River

San Joaquin River

YOSEMITE NATIONAL PARK

Mono Lake

NEVADA

n Francisco Bay

San Francisco

Farallon Islands

KINGS CANYON NATIONAL PARK

INYO NATIONAL FOREST

Monterey Bay

Salinas River

San Joaquin Valley

SEQUOIA NATIONAL PARK

Kern River

DEATH VALLEY NATIONAL PARK

Colorado River

Pacific Ocean

COAST RANGES

AZ

Mojave Desert

JOSHUA TREE NATIONAL MONUMENT

Santa Barbara Channel

Los Angeles

San Jacinto Mts.

PENINSULAR RANGES

Santa Cruz Island

Colorado River

Santa Catalina Island

Salton Sea

Jacumba Mts.

ANZA-BORREGO DESERT STATE PARK

San Diego

MEXICO

N

= Sierra Nevada bighorns

= Desert bighorns

Bighorn Sheep Facts

▶ **Endangered Bighorns**

Ovis canadensis nelsoni, desert bighorn sheep in the Peninsular Ranges of southern California, is currently listed as endangered by the United States Fish and Wildlife Service (USFWS). *Ovis canadensis sierrae,* a different subspecies of bighorn sheep, occupies the southern and central Sierra Nevada of California and is also listed as endangered.

▶ **Most Recent Population Estimates**

Desert bighorns in Peninsular Ranges, 700 as of 2004

Sierra Nevada bighorns, 350–400 as of 2006

▶ **Area of Habitation**

Desert bighorn sheep in the Peninsular Ranges of California live in a string of desert ranges in Riverside, San Diego, and Imperial counties from the San Jacinto Mountains south to the Jacumba Mountains near the border with Mexico, a distance of about 100 miles (160 kilometers). Sierra Nevada bighorns live along about 150 miles (250 kilometers) of the crest and east side of the southern and central Sierra Nevada in western Inyo and Mono counties and eastern Tulare, Fresno, and Tuolumne counties, mostly on lands managed by the U.S. Forest Service and National Park Service. This land includes three national forests and two national parks.

▶ **Types of Habitats**

High, rugged mountains, steep cliffs, canyons, deserts

▶ **Life Span**

Ewes, about 18 years; rams, about 12

▶ **Average Size**

4 $\frac{1}{2}$ to 6 $\frac{1}{2}$ feet (125 to 180 centimeters) long; 40 inches (101 centimeters) tall at the shoulders

▶ Weight (average)

Desert rams: 180 pounds (82 kilograms)

Desert ewes: 120 pounds (54 kilograms)

Mountain rams: 285 pounds (129 kilograms)

Mountain ewes: 136 pounds (62 kilograms)

▶ Most Notable Feature

Rams have massive, curved horns; ewes have smaller horns.

▶ Diet

Bighorn sheep are herbivorous and eat a great variety of plants depending on the season.

▶ Sensory Systems

Very sharp eyesight, equal to eight-power binoculars

▶ Locomotion

The structure of the bighorns' hooves and relatively short legs, producing a low center of gravity, enable the sheep to have amazing rock-climbing ability.

▶ Communication

Desert ewes and lambs vocalize a lot to communicate, and rams in the rut (the period when they are sexually excited and looking to mate) have a low-pitched growl. Sierra ewes and lambs rarely vocalize, but rams in rut growl.

▶ Reproduction

The gestation period is about six months. Ewes usually give birth to one lamb at a time. In the Sierra Nevada, the mating season occurs in fall and early winter with lambs born from mid-April through June. In the Peninsular Ranges, the mating season is in summer and early fall, with births occurring in winter and spring and about 5 percent of the time in summer.

The wild sheep ranks among the noblest of animal mountaineers. Possessed of keen sight, immovable nerve, and strong limbs, he dwells secure amid the loftiest summits of the Sierra. . . . developing from generation to generation in perfect strength and beauty.

John Muir

KINGS OF THE CRAGS

The bighorn sheep (*Ovis canadensis*) is one of two species of North American wild sheep. The thinhorn sheep (*Ovis dalli*) is the other. Bighorns inhabit various environments in the mountains and deserts of western North America. These magnificent animals with their large, curved horns have long been admired for their beauty and agility. Those who come across bighorns in their native habitat never fail to be amazed by their ability to bound up and down mountainsides that seem impossibly steep to navigate.

John Muir, the famous nineteenth-century naturalist and conservationist who is often referred to as the father of our national park system, saw bighorn sheep while exploring California's Sierra Nevada. That mountain range, which runs for nearly 400 miles (640 kilometers) mostly through the eastern part of the state, is home to three national parks, including Yosemite. Muir expressed his admiration for the bighorns of the Sierra Nevada in his essay "The Wild Sheep of California."

▲ John Muir, right, and President Theodore Roosevelt, both committed to the conservation of America's wild places and wildlife, stand on Glacier Point, in the Yosemite Valley of California, in a photograph from 1906. Muir marveled at the amazing strength and grace of the bighorns he saw in Yosemite.

In California, the wild sheep ranks among the noblest of animal mountaineers. Possessed of keen sight, immovable nerve, and strong limbs, he dwells secure amid the loftiest summits of the Sierra, leaping unscathed from crag to crag, crossing foaming torrents and slopes of frozen snow, exposed to the wildest storms, yet maintaining a brave life, and developing from generation to generation in perfect strength and beauty.[1]

In that essay, Muir marveled at the climbing skills of three bighorns he observed: "Presently, they made a dash at a steep ice-polished incline, and reached the top without a struggle, by a succession of short, stiff leaps, bringing their hoofs down sharply with a patting sound. This was the most astounding feat of mountaineering I had ever witnessed."[2]

A bighorn ram, one of the "kings of the crags" in Rocky Mountain National Park.

▶ Endangered Bighorns

The United States Fish and Wildlife Service (USFWS), charged with protecting America's endangered animals and plants, currently lists two bighorn sheep subspecies in North America as endangered. *Ovis canadensis nelsoni,* a population of desert bighorn sheep, are endangered in the Peninsular Ranges of southern California. *Ovis canadensis sierrae* (formerly referred to as *Ovis canadensis californiana*), Sierra Nevada bighorn sheep that live only in the southern and central Sierra Nevada, are also endangered. *Ovis* means "sheep" in Latin, while *canadensis* means "of Canada."

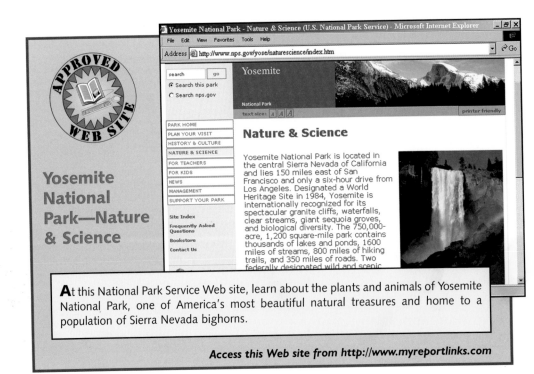

Yosemite National Park—Nature & Science

At this National Park Service Web site, learn about the plants and animals of Yosemite National Park, one of America's most beautiful natural treasures and home to a population of Sierra Nevada bighorns.

Access this Web site from http://www.myreportlinks.com

At one time, there were many bighorn sheep in the mountains and deserts of North America. Estimates of the bighorn population in the 1800s range from a half million to about 2 million. Since then, there has been a drastic reduction in the bighorn population. According to the U.S. Fish and Wildlife Service, the population of the desert bighorn in the Peninsular Ranges as of 2004, which was estimated through aerial surveys by helicopter, is 700. Even more alarming, the Sierra Nevada bighorn came close to becoming extinct. In 1995, there were only 100 of them remaining in their mountain habitat. But their numbers have since increased, reaching 350 to 400 by 2006.

▶ The Endangered Species Act of 1973

Because of threats to their continued existence, those subspecies of bighorn sheep have been classified as endangered. In 1973, the United States Congress passed the Endangered Species Act (ESA), the most far-reaching conservation law in American history. The law's purpose was "to provide a means whereby the ecosystems upon which endangered species and threatened species depend may be conserved, to provide a program for the conservation of such endangered species and threatened species."[3] Although earlier acts had been passed to try to save animals that were threatened with extinction, they provided only limited protection. The Endangered Species Act of 1973 combined the provisions of the earlier acts and considerably strengthened the protection given to native and nonnative species. It prohibited any government action that harmed species at risk and authorized the acquisition of land to protect such species.

The Endangered Species Act defines an endangered species as one that is in immediate danger of becoming extinct throughout most of its range. Threatened species are defined as those that could become endangered in the near future. In 1973, the federal list of endangered species consisted of seventy-seven species. As of November 2006,

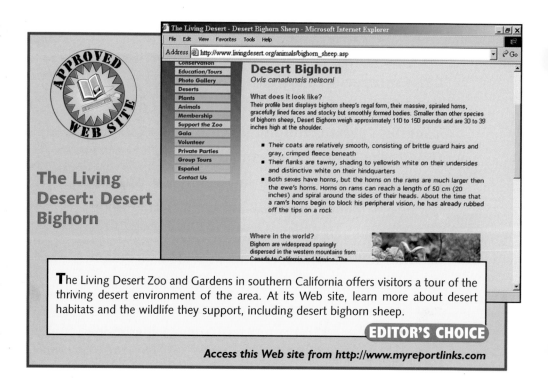

The Living Desert: Desert Bighorn

The Living Desert - Desert Bighorn Sheep - Microsoft Internet Explorer

File Edit View Favorites Tools Help

Address http://www.livingdesert.org/animals/bighorn_sheep.asp

Conservation
Education/Tours
Photo Gallery
Deserts
Plants
Animals
Membership
Support the Zoo
Gala
Volunteer
Private Parties
Group Tours
Español
Contact Us

Desert Bighorn
Ovis canadensis nelsoni

What does it look like?
Their profile best displays bighorn sheep's regal form, their massive, spiraled horns, gracefully lined faces and stocky but smoothly formed bodies. Smaller than other species of bighorn sheep, Desert Bighorn weigh approximately 110 to 150 pounds and are 30 to 39 inches high at the shoulder.

- Their coats are relatively smooth, consisting of brittle guard hairs and gray, crimped fleece beneath
- Their flanks are tawny, shading to yellowish white on their undersides and distinctive white on their hindquarters
- Both sexes have horns, but the horns on the rams are much larger then the ewe's horns. Horns on rams can reach a length of 50 cm (20 inches) and spiral around the sides of their heads. About the time that a ram's horns begin to block his peripheral vision, he has already rubbed off the tips on a rock

Where in the world?
Bighorn are widespread sparingly dispersed in the western mountains from Canada to California and Mexico. The

The Living Desert Zoo and Gardens in southern California offers visitors a tour of the thriving desert environment of the area. At its Web site, learn more about desert habitats and the wildlife they support, including desert bighorn sheep.

EDITOR'S CHOICE

Access this Web site from http://www.myreportlinks.com

1,009 animal and plant species were listed as endangered, and 302 species were listed as threatened. In addition, thousands more are considered "species of concern" or "critically imperiled" by states, environmental groups, and scientists.

Meanwhile, the IUCN-World Conservation Union has been maintaining its own list of endangered species. In May 2006, the IUCN released an update of its Red List of Threatened Species. More than 40 percent (16,119 species) of the 40,177 species assessed by the IUCN are threatened with extinction. These include one in four mammals, one in eight birds, one in three amphibians, and a quarter of the world's coniferous trees.

State Protections Lead to Federal Ones

In 1971, the state of California first designated the desert bighorn in the Peninsular Ranges as a "rare animal." In 1984, the designation was changed to "threatened." On March 18, 1998, the U.S. Fish and Wildlife Service, the federal government agency that oversees the Endangered Species Act, listed the desert bighorn in the Peninsular Ranges as endangered. A recovery plan was then drafted in which the agency identified habitat loss as the major threat to the desert bighorns in the Peninsular Ranges. The plan includes proposals to ensure the survival of this population of sheep.

▲ A bighorn ram looks out over the landscape from a mountain cliff.

The Sierra Nevada bighorn sheep subspecies was first temporarily listed as endangered on April 20, 1999, through an emergency rule, when its numbers had become so low. Because of predators and disease, there were only about one hundred sheep, in five isolated herds, remaining.

One of the reasons that conservationists sought federal protection for the Sierra Nevada bighorns had to do, ironically, with another conservation act. In 1990, voters in California passed a law called the Wildlife Protection Act. That law prevented the California Department of Fish and Game from protecting threatened and endangered species, such as bighorn sheep, from mountain lions, since the new law also protected mountain lions. By helping one population, the state had unintentionally harmed another.

In 1999, the California legislature made changes to the Wildlife Protection Act. It allowed officials with the state to remove mountain lions that were seen as an immediate threat to bighorn sheep populations. On January 3, 2000, the Sierra Nevada subspecies was finally listed as federally endangered.[4]

▷ Why Bighorn Populations Have Plummeted

Bighorns were among the most highly prized of all big-game species in North America. Hunters were attracted by the great curling horns of bighorn rams, and the high mountain habitat of the animals provided an irresistible challenge to sportsmen. As a result, during the past one hundred years, bighorns were almost hunted to extinction. Today, hunting of bighorns is tightly regulated by the various states with bighorn populations. But poaching, or illegal hunting, of bighorns continues to be a problem. Bighorns are also killed by nonhuman hunters. These natural predators include mountain lions, wolves, coyotes, bears, golden eagles, bobcats, and lynx.

Bighorns face other problems as well, especially loss of habitat. In various places, humans are encroaching on the bighorns' habitat. Mining and agricultural activities have expanded into

Bighorn Sheep Threatened by Climate Change

A decline in the population of California's desert bighorn sheep is linked to climate change by researchers at the University of California, Berkeley. Read about conservationists' fears that bighorns could become extinct because of global warming.

Access this Web site from http://www.myreportlinks.com

areas that had previously been wilderness. Between 1991 and 1996, in the Santa Rosa Mountains south of Palm Springs, California, five desert bighorns were killed when they were struck by automobiles. Another one strangled itself in a wire fence, and bighorn lambs have been known to drown in swimming pools.

The bighorns' habitat is also threatened by changes to the environment. Among these threats are changes to the local vegetation and drying up of available sources of water. These changes are thought to be caused by global warming. According to a study in 2004 on desert bighorns in California, a temperature increase of 3.6°F in the next sixty years accompanied by a 12 percent decrease in precipitation will result in a 30 percent chance that the desert bighorns will become extinct in southern California. According to one of the study's authors, Clinton W. Epps, a University of California, Berkeley, graduate student, "Our study illustrates how sensitive certain populations can be to changes in climate, whether man-made or not. Cases like this give conservationists some ammunition when talking about the importance of controlling global warming."[5]

Bighorns are also threatened by diseases such as scabies (a contagious itch or mange caused by mites) and pneumonia, which are carried by domestic sheep. In various places, domestic livestock graze on lands that used to be the exclusive habitat of wild bighorn sheep.

How You Can Help

One of the most useful things you can do to help protect not only bighorn sheep but also other endangered species is to show your support for the Endangered Species Act. Currently, certain members of Congress are trying to weaken the act or even do away with it altogether. The Sierra Club, America's oldest and largest environmental organization, founded by John Muir in 1892, contains the following petition on its Web site. Although bighorn sheep are not specifically mentioned in this petition, as federally listed

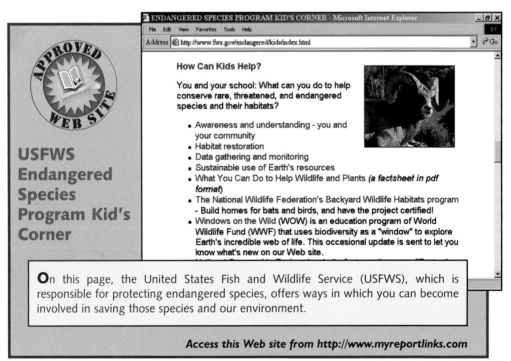

USFWS Endangered Species Program Kid's Corner

ENDANGERED SPECIES PROGRAM KID'S CORNER - Microsoft Internet Explorer

File Edit View Favorites Tools Help

Address http://www.fws.gov/endangered/kids/index.html

How Can Kids Help?

You and your school: What can you do to help conserve rare, threatened, and endangered species and their habitats?

- Awareness and understanding - you and your community
- Habitat restoration
- Data gathering and monitoring
- Sustainable use of Earth's resources
- What You Can Do to Help Wildlife and Plants (*a factsheet in pdf format*)
- The National Wildlife Federation's Backyard Wildlife Habitats program - Build homes for bats and birds, and have the project certified!
- Windows on the Wild (WOW) is an education program of World Wildlife Fund (WWF) that uses biodiversity as a "window" to explore Earth's incredible web of life. This occasional update is sent to let you know what's new on our Web site.

On this page, the United States Fish and Wildlife Service (USFWS), which is responsible for protecting endangered species, offers ways in which you can become involved in saving those species and our environment.

Access this Web site from http://www.myreportlinks.com

endangered species, they still need the protections provided by the act, now more than ever. You can add your voice to many others who are urging our elected members of Congress to save the Endangered Species Act. Invite your family and friends to sign this petition also.

> I am writing to urge you to reject the House of Representatives' legislation that would undermine America's premier wildlife protection law. The Endangered Species Act is a great success story, helping species on the brink of extinction to recover. I urge you to make sure that clear, enforceable standards for the protection of habitat remain part of a strong Endangered Species Act.
>
> We need to protect more wildlife habitat, not weaken the Endangered Species Act. Rather than rewriting the Endangered Species Act, Congress should be finding ways to set aside more land for wildlife habitat and establishing new National Wildlife Refuges to provide habitat for species like the grizzly bear, salmon, sage grouse, and jaguar. Thank you for your continued leadership on this important issue.[6]

If you prefer, you can send elected officials an e-mail directly. Go to the *Write Your Representative* link for this book on **www.myreportlinks.com** to find out the names of the people representing your district and their e-mail addresses.

Another way to help endangered bighorn sheep is to write a letter to the editor of your local newspaper. In the letter, point out that the

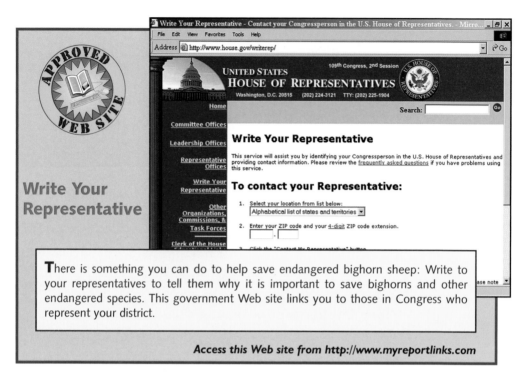

There is something you can do to help save endangered bighorn sheep: Write to your representatives to tell them why it is important to save bighorns and other endangered species. This government Web site links you to those in Congress who represent your district.

Access this Web site from http://www.myreportlinks.com

Endangered Species Act works very effectively to protect endangered species. Stress that you believe Congress should work to strengthen the law rather than weaken it. The Endangered Species Act has prevented 99 percent of all the wildlife, fish, and plants placed under its care from going extinct, and it has helped secure a future for hundreds of native plants and animals. Many species, such as the desert bighorn sheep, have seen dramatic increases in their population since they were listed, and now are on the road to recovery.

▶ Other Groups Working to Protect Bighorns

Many organizations are specifically working to preserve and increase populations of bighorn sheep. These nonprofit organizations often hold fund-raising activities and welcome donations. You can contribute any amount of money—a $5 donation is just as as welcome as a $5,000 donation. You and your class could also hold fund-raising events and donate the proceeds to a bighorn sheep conservation organization, such as the following.

- The Sierra Nevada Bighorn Sheep Foundation has as its mission the conservation of that subspecies by bringing its situation to the attention of government agencies. The foundation is also strongly committed to educating the public about this subspecies of bighorn and its struggle to survive.

- The Bighorn Institute promotes the conservation of wild sheep. It supports research, particularly projects involving the desert bighorn of southern California.

- The Foundation for North American Wild Sheep (FNAWS) provides financial support wherever bighorn sheep are in danger. FNAWS also funds scientific studies on population statistics, herd quality, and water-hole restoration, as well as research into bighorn genetics. The scientific research is extremely expensive. Although the members of FNAWS are dedicated to preserving and restoring bighorn sheep, they are also hunters, and a large portion of the money they raise comes from the auction of bighorn hunting permits.

Sierra Nevada Bighorn Sheep Foundation

The Sierra Nevada Bighorn Sheep Foundation, which helped bring the plight of these sheep to the public's attention, is dedicated to saving the subspecies. Learn more about the group's efforts and history at its Web site.

EDITOR'S CHOICE

Access this Web site from http://www.myreportlinks.com

Go to **www.myreportlinks.com** to link to the Web sites of these organizations.

Other bighorn sheep conservation organizations include the Society for the Conservation of Bighorn Sheep, the National Bighorn Sheep Interpretive Center, the Arizona Desert Bighorn Sheep Society, the Rocky Mountain Bighorn Sheep Society, the Texas Bighorn Society, and the Wild Sheep Society of British Columbia in Port Coquitlam, British Columbia.

Another way to help protect endangered bighorn sheep is to set up an information table at your school to tell people about the threat of extinction facing bighorns. Gather information

▲ *The key to saving endangered species, such as bighorn sheep, is getting people to care about the animals first by learning as much as they can about them.*

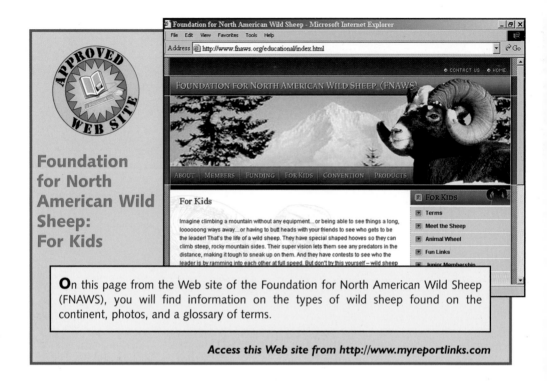

Foundation for North American Wild Sheep: For Kids

FOUNDATION FOR NORTH AMERICAN WILD SHEEP (FNAWS)

ABOUT | MEMBERS | FUNDING | FOR KIDS | CONVENTION | PRODUCTS

For Kids

Imagine climbing a mountain without any equipment...or being able to see things a long, looooong ways away...or having to butt heads with your friends to see who gets to be the leader! That's the life of a wild sheep. They have special shaped hooves so they can climb steep, rocky mountain sides. Their super vision lets them see any predators in the distance, making it tough to sneak up on them. And they have contests to see who the leader is by ramming into each other at full speed. But don't try this yourself – wild sheep

FOR KIDS
- Terms
- Meet the Sheep
- Animal Wheel
- Fun Links
- Junior Membership

On this page from the Web site of the Foundation for North American Wild Sheep (FNAWS), you will find information on the types of wild sheep found on the continent, photos, and a glossary of terms.

Access this Web site from http://www.myreportlinks.com

about bighorn sheep from these organizations. It is only through caring about wildlife and letting others know why they should care too that people can make a difference in saving the species of our world, including the majestic bighorn sheep.

Protect the Planet

Finally, you can help endangered bighorns as well as other endangered species by becoming a good steward of the earth. That means, first of all, realizing that every action you and others take to help keep our rivers and air as clean as they can possibly be also contributes to the welfare of the animals who share our planet. Recycle as many

Snow-capped peaks of the Sierra Nevada rise above farmland in Mono County, California, which is home to endangered Sierra Nevada bighorns.

products as you can; encourage your parents to use organic products rather than harmful chemicals in lawn care; and help to educate as many people as you can about the importance of saving species. When one species dies out, all other species are affected by that loss, whether directly or indirectly. When habitats are lost, all of the species that depend on those habitats, including us, are affected. When ecosystems are damaged, the animal and plant life within them become less diverse. When people begin to think of themselves as part of the natural world, they will become more likely to think of themselves as its guardians rather than its masters, and we will all benefit.

Chapter 2 ▶

ORIGIN, HABITATS, AND DISTRIBUTION OF BIGHORN SHEEP

Scientists who study the fossil record of bighorn sheep have determined that they originated in Asia, not North America. Wild sheep first began migrating to North America about one million years ago.

Scientists refer to this geological time period as the Pleistocene era. There was a series of four ice ages during that period of the earth's history. Several times during each ice age, vast ice sheets formed in northern latitudes. Seawaters froze, and glaciers advanced over land. Sea levels dropped 300 to 400 feet (91 to 122 meters). A land bridge called Beringia emerged from the Bering Strait, which separates Asia from North America. Wild animals migrated across this 50-mile-long (80-kilometer-long) land bridge connecting eastern Siberia and Alaska.

Ancestors of today's wild mountain sheep were among the first animal species to cross the Beringia land bridge. Following them came the ancestors of today's goats, deer, moose, elk, musk

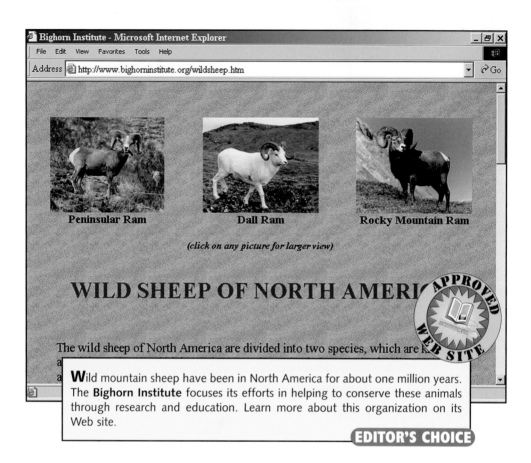

Peninsular Ram   Dall Ram   Rocky Mountain Ram

(click on any picture for larger view)

WILD SHEEP OF NORTH AMERI

The wild sheep of North America are divided into two species, which are

Wild mountain sheep have been in North America for about one million years. The **Bighorn Institute** focuses its efforts in helping to conserve these animals through research and education. Learn more about this organization on its Web site.

EDITOR'S CHOICE

oxen, and bison. Much later, possibly beginning about thirty-five thousand years ago during the most recent ice age, humans migrated across the land bridge from Asia. They were nomadic hunters following the herds of wild animals.

▷ Evolution of Bighorn Sheep

Scientists believe that sometime during the early Pleistocene period, there was a common ancestor of mountain sheep and goats. At some point, two separate species evolved. But the fossil evidence is too sparse to give scientists a precise picture of when the two diverged. Very few fossil specimens have been found. In the typical bighorn habitat amidst steep, rocky cliffs, moving rock rubble eventually crushes all bone.

Some of the mountain sheep to reach Alaska remained in northwestern Alaska. Others moved southward as the glaciers retreated with the ending of each ice age. These sheep were bighorn sheep. When the climate cooled again and the glaciers advanced once more, the bighorns that had roamed south were blocked from moving back up north. Later groups of mountain sheep to arrive in North America stayed in Alaska. Parts of northwestern Alaska remained free of ice, but glaciers blocked the way south.

Glaciers and Movement

The most recent group of mountain sheep crossed the Beringia land bridge about ten thousand years ago. Glaciers still blocked the way south, so the new arrivals mixed with the bighorns that had remained in Alaska. These mountain sheep in the northern latitudes evolved separately into the thinhorns. The Peace River valley in western Canada became the boundary between the two distinct species of mountain sheep. Meanwhile, the bighorns spread throughout western North America and roamed as far south as Baja

California, a Mexican peninsula, and the northern part of the Mexican mainland.

Habitats and Distribution

Wild mountain sheep live in a wide variety of habitats in the western mountains and deserts of North America. A vast arc of their habitat extends all the way from Asia across the Bering Strait to North America. The arc then sweeps southward down the mountain ranges of Alaska and Canada and into the western United States. The arc finally ends in the mountains of Mexico's Baja California and Sonora.

The thinhorn sheep in the north inhabit the Brooks and Alaska ranges in Alaska and the Rocky

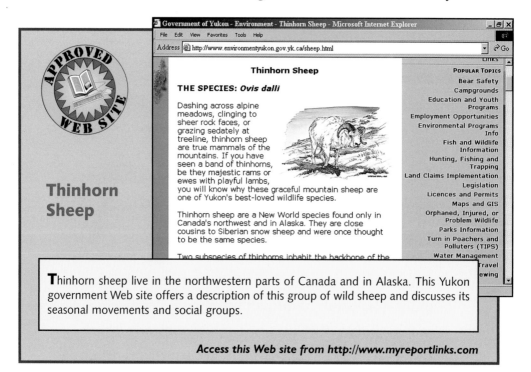

Thinhorn Sheep

Government of Yukon - Environment - Thinhorn Sheep - Microsoft Internet Explorer

File   Edit   View   Favorites   Tools   Help

Address   http://www.environmentyukon.gov.yk.ca/sheep.html

Thinhorn Sheep

THE SPECIES: *Ovis dalli*

Dashing across alpine meadows, clinging to sheer rock faces, or grazing sedately at treeline, thinhorn sheep are true mammals of the mountains. If you have seen a band of thinhorns, be they majestic rams or ewes with playful lambs, you will know why these graceful mountain sheep are one of Yukon's best-loved wildlife species.

Thinhorn sheep are a New World species found only in Canada's northwest and in Alaska. They are close cousins to Siberian snow sheep and were once thought to be the same species.

Two subspecies of thinhorns inhabit the backbone of the

LINKS

POPULAR TOPICS
Bear Safety
Campgrounds
Education and Youth Programs
Employment Opportunities
Environmental Programs Info
Fish and Wildlife Information
Hunting, Fishing and Trapping
Land Claims Implementation
Legislation
Licences and Permits
Maps and GIS
Orphaned, Injured, or Problem Wildlife
Parks Information
Turn in Poachers and Polluters (TIPS)
Water Management
Travel
ewing

Thinhorn sheep live in the northwestern parts of Canada and in Alaska. This Yukon government Web site offers a description of this group of wild sheep and discusses its seasonal movements and social groups.

Access this Web site from http://www.myreportlinks.com

Mountains in Canada. There are three subspecies of thinhorn sheep—Dall sheep, Stone sheep, and Kenai Peninsula Dall sheep. As the name suggests, the horns of these sheep are not as massive as those of the bighorns. Thinhorns have horns that average 12.5 inches (32 centimeters) at the base. Bighorns have horns that measure up to 17 inches (43 centimeters) around at the base.

▶ Classifying Bighorns

Today, most scientists agree that North American bighorn sheep can be divided into two types depending on their habitat: mountain bighorns and desert bighorns. But it has only been recently that scientists have come to refer to only two distinct subspecies of bighorn sheep, the Sierra Nevada bighorns and the desert bighorns. Improved research methods have changed, and may continue to change, how bighorns are classified.

The Sierra Nevada bighorns, formerly called the California bighorns, live in the southern and central Sierra Nevada of California. Desert bighorns can be found in mountain and desert environments throughout the west, from British Columbia down to northern Mexico. Mountain-dwelling bighorns live at elevations that range from 1,500 to 10,800 feet (457 to 3,292 meters) above sea level. Desert bighorns in California inhabit an even wider range of elevations. Some can

Rocky Mountain Bighorn Sheep -- Enlarged Animal Photo, Wallpapers -- National Geographic - Microsof...

File   Edit   View   Favorites   Tools   Help

Address   http://www3.nationalgeographic.com/animals/enlarge/rocky-mountain-bighorn-sheep.html

A mountain bighorn ram lowers its head. This image and others can be found on *National Geographic:* **Rocky Mountain Bighorn Sheep,** which also includes a video clip of rams in a clash, butting horns.

be found 256 feet (78 meters) below sea level in California's Death Valley. Others live at elevations of up to 14,000 feet (4,267 meters) in the White Mountains of California.

In 1940, the naturalist I. McT. Cowan, who had been studying bighorn sheep in their natural habitats, split the bighorn species into seven subspecies: California bighorns, desert (Nelson's) bighorns, Rocky Mountain bighorns, Mexican bighorns, Weems' bighorns, peninsular bighorns, and Audubon's bighorns.[1] But in 1993, John

D. Wehausen, Rob R. Ramey II, and their colleagues showed through DNA testing that the division of bighorns into seven subspecies was not correct.[2] It is true that there are minor physical variations between the seven groups, which is why Cowan and others had considered them to be separate subspecies. But Ramey's genetics research showed that there are only two genetically distinct subspecies of bighorns.

The six types of desert bighorns are genetically identical. The desert bighorns developed different physical characteristics in order to adapt to their particular environments. Those that dwell in the mountains weigh more than their desert-dwelling cousins. The desert-dwelling bighorns have longer teeth, broader noses, and longer ears than the mountain dwellers. The desert bighorns' coats are paler than those of the mountain bighorns.

▷ Environmental Impact

Jeff Grandison, a wildlife program coordinator in Cedar City, Utah, learned just how much power the land has to influence the physical characteristics of bighorn sheep. He took desert bighorns, moved them from their desert habitat, and relocated them in an area in the mountains previously inhabited by Rocky Mountain bighorns. Within a few years, Grandison noticed that the desert bighorns had all the characteristics of the Rocky

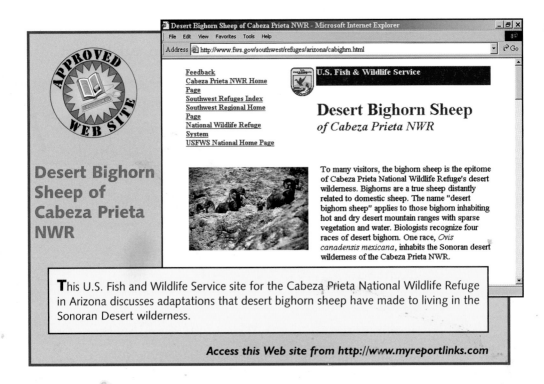

Desert Bighorn Sheep of Cabeza Prieta NWR - Microsoft Internet Explorer

File   Edit   View   Favorites   Tools   Help

Address http://www.fws.gov/southwest/refuges/arizona/cabighrn.html   Go

Feedback
Cabeza Prieta NWR Home
Page
Southwest Refuges Index
Southwest Regional Home
Page
National Wildlife Refuge
System
USFWS National Home Page

U.S. Fish & Wildlife Service

Desert Bighorn Sheep
of Cabeza Prieta NWR

To many visitors, the bighorn sheep is the epitome of Cabeza Prieta National Wildlife Refuge's desert wilderness. Bighorns are a true sheep distantly related to domestic sheep. The name "desert bighorn sheep" applies to those bighorn inhabiting hot and dry desert mountain ranges with sparse vegetation and water. Biologists recognize four races of desert bighorn. One race, *Ovis canadensis mexicana*, inhabits the Sonoran desert wilderness of the Cabeza Prieta NWR.

Desert Bighorn Sheep of Cabeza Prieta NWR

This U.S. Fish and Wildlife Service site for the Cabeza Prieta National Wildlife Refuge in Arizona discusses adaptations that desert bighorn sheep have made to living in the Sonoran Desert wilderness.

Access this Web site from http://www.myreportlinks.com

Mountain bighorns. According to Grandison, "The point is that the country shapes the sheep."[3]

Home on the Range

The area of land used by animals throughout their lives is called their home range. The bighorns' overall home range consists of seasonal ranges within it. The bighorn herd moves from one part of the home range to another depending on the season. Mountain bighorns spend the summers at the highest elevations in their home range. In the fall, they migrate to lower elevations because food is available there. Each year, the bighorns return to the same seasonal ranges.

▲ A bighorn ram against the backdrop of its mountainous habitat. Mountain bighorns require a larger range than desert bighorns do.

The home range may vary for rams and ewes and for old sheep and young sheep. While rams and ewes can manage with just two seasonal ranges—summer and winter—they usually need a greater variety of areas for specific activities. Rams need a prerut range, a rutting range, a spring range, and a salt-lick range in addition to a winter range and a summer range. Ewes need a spring range and a lambing range besides the winter and summer ranges.

The size of the home range varies. It all depends on environmental factors such as snow cover in the north and availability of water in the desert. The movement of bighorns within their home range also varies. Observers have reported that bighorns in the desert may never move more than 5 to 10 miles (8 to 16 kilometers) from their place of birth. Bighorns in the mountains in Idaho have been known to migrate as far as 40 miles (64 kilometers) from their summer ranges to their winter ranges.[4]

PHYSICAL CHARACTERISTICS OF BIGHORN SHEEP

"Monarchs of the high country" and "kings of the crags" are phrases often used to describe bighorn sheep. For many lovers of the wilderness, the bighorns with their regal bearing seem to symbolize the majesty and beauty of the mountains. These amazing creatures have unique physical attributes that allow them to survive in their remote, rugged habitats.

▶ Bighorn Sheep Are "Big"

Bighorns are considered to be "big" animals. Most bighorns are 4 1/2 to 6 feet (125 to 180 centimeters) long. They are about 40 inches (102 centimeters) tall at the shoulders. Adult male bighorns, or rams, weigh more than adult female bighorns, or ewes. And mountain dwellers weigh more than desert dwellers. A mountain bighorn ram will usually weigh 285 pounds (129 kilograms). Mountain rams occasionally weigh as much as 300 pounds (136 kilograms) or more. This compares to the 180-pound (82-kilogram) average weight of a desert-dwelling ram. The

▲ *A mountain ram in Rocky Mountain National Park, Colorado. Male mountain bighorns are the largest of all bighorn sheep, sometimes reaching six feet in length.*

mountain-dwelling bighorn ewe weighs 136 pounds (62 kilograms) on average, versus 120 pounds (54 kilograms) for the desert bighorn ewe. Amazingly, these large animals with their massive horns are not only nimble on their feet as they scamper up and down the slopes, but they are also good swimmers.

Scientists believe there is a reason for the difference in bighorn weights. It all has to do with how the animal has evolved to survive in its habitat. A nineteenth-century German biologist, Christian Bergmann, theorized that an animal living in a cold climate, like that of the high mountain country where bighorns live, withstands the cold better by having a larger body. This principle of zoology has come to be called Bergmann's Rule. A large body loses less heat proportionally than a smaller body. Meanwhile, in a hot desert environment, a smaller body can more easily get rid of body heat.

▶ The Effect of Habitat

Habitat also has an effect on the physical appearance of bighorn sheep. Bighorns have thick brown coats with white patches on the rump, the muzzle, and the back of the hind legs. Unlike the wool coat of domestic sheep, the bighorn's coat consists of coarse hair, like that of a deer. The coats of desert-dwelling sheep tend to be lighter than those of the

ADW: bighorn2306.jpg - Microsoft Internet Explorer

File   Edit   View   Favorites   Tools   Help

Address http://animaldiversity.ummz.umich.edu/site/resources/phil_myers/ADW_mammals_3_4_03/bighorn2306.jp   Go

All bighorns have horns, but only the adult rams, like this one pictured in Glacier National Park, Montana, bear the huge curved horns that the species has come to be known for. This image is from **ADW: *Ovis canadensis*,** a Web site of the University of Michigan Museum of Zoology.

mountain dwellers. According to another rule of zoology, Gloger's Rule, animals living in dry environments, such as deserts, tend to be lighter colored than those living in humid forests. Some scientists believe that the difference in color has to do with camouflage. The lighter color of desert sheep helps them to blend in with their desert environment. This enables them to be less visible to hungry predators. The lighter color may also have to do with bleaching in high altitudes and in deserts from exposure to the sun.

About Those Horns

At one time, some people used to believe that the bighorns' horns were so strong that the sheep were able to descend a mountain safely and quickly by jumping off a cliff and landing on their horns. Of course, this was not true—although the horns are indeed strong. A skeptical John Muir wrote that the bighorn sheep

> is said to plunge fearlessly down the faces of sheer precipices, and alight on his huge elastic horns. I know only two hunters who claim to have witnessed this feat; I never was so fortunate. They describe the act as a diving head-foremost. Some of the horns that I have examined with reference to this question are certainly much battered in front, and are so large at the base that they cover all the upper portion of the head down nearly to a level with the eyes; moreover, the skull of a wild sheep is stronger than a bull's.[1]

Muir went on to say that although rock diving might not cause the bighorns' skulls to fracture, the other bones might get broken.

All adult bighorns, male and female, have horns. But only the adult male, or ram, has the huge curved horns the species is known for. The characteristic big horn of the ram coils backward and then forward again. The horns of the mountain-dwelling sheep are bigger than those of the desert dwellers. Horn lengths of over three-and-a-half feet (one meter) are typical of mountain

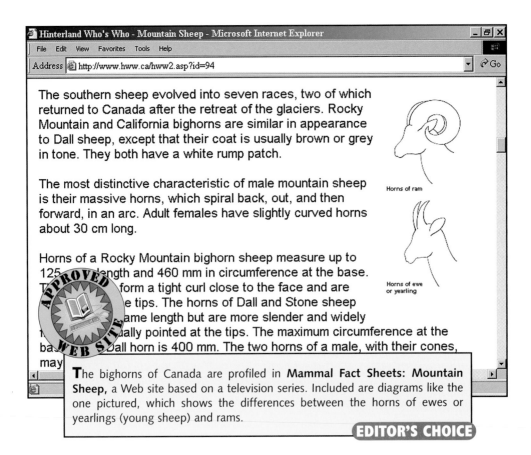

Hinterland Who's Who - Mountain Sheep - Microsoft Internet Explorer

File   Edit   View   Favorites   Tools   Help

Address   http://www.hww.ca/hww2.asp?id=94   Go

The southern sheep evolved into seven races, two of which returned to Canada after the retreat of the glaciers. Rocky Mountain and California bighorns are similar in appearance to Dall sheep, except that their coat is usually brown or grey in tone. They both have a white rump patch.

The most distinctive characteristic of male mountain sheep is their massive horns, which spiral back, out, and then forward, in an arc. Adult females have slightly curved horns about 30 cm long.

Horns of ram

Horns of a Rocky Mountain bighorn sheep measure up to 125 ___ length and 460 mm in circumference at the base. T___ form a tight curl close to the face and are ___ e tips. The horns of Dall and Stone sheep ___ ame length but are more slender and widely ___ ally pointed at the tips. The maximum circumference at the ba___ Dall horn is 400 mm. The two horns of a male, with their cones, may

Horns of ewe or yearling

The bighorns of Canada are profiled in **Mammal Fact Sheets: Mountain Sheep,** a Web site based on a television series. Included are diagrams like the one pictured, which shows the differences between the horns of ewes or yearlings (young sheep) and rams.

EDITOR'S CHOICE

rams, and the horns can weigh as much as 45 pounds (20 kilograms). Although the horn of the ewe is also curved, it is usually less than a foot (.3 meter) long. A ewe's horn usually weighs four to five pounds (1.8 to 2.2 kilograms).

The sheep's horn consists of two layers. A short bony core is attached to the skull. Covering this is a keratin sheath, which makes up most of the horn. Keratin is a tough protein, the same substance human fingernails are made of. Bighorns never shed their horns, the way that deer, elk, and moose shed their antlers each year, but rams do break their horns during combat. The horns grow throughout the bighorn's life, which for ewes averages eighteen years and rams twelve years. How fast these horns grow depends on several factors, including diet and the mineral content of the soil. During a bighorn's first year, the horns grow about twelve inches (thirty centimeters). They continue to grow each year. But from the age of seven or eight on, there is little growth.

No Two Horns Alike

Each winter, the sheep's horns stop growing. A deep groove on the horn known as an annular ring forms. Scientists can tell the age of a bighorn by the number of growth rings on its horns. Rams often blunt their horns by rubbing the tips against rocks and trees. This wearing down of the tips of the horn is called "brooming." Rams also broom off horns during fights.

Scientists studying bighorns believe that no two horns are alike. Just as humans can be identified by their fingerprints, so can bighorns be identified by the uniqueness of their horns. Scientists look for the tightness of the curl of the horn, the spread of the horns, and the degree of brooming. They note features such as chips, nicks, breaks, and the degree of ridging, which make each horn distinct.

Three bighorns in Canada's Banff National Park, Alberta. Writer Bert Gildart and his wife were amazed by the thousands of sure-footed sheep tracks they came across in that park, signs of the species' incredible rock-climbing abilities.

▷ Agile Climbers

For nature writer and photographer Bert Gildart, sheep tracks in the mountains provided evidence of the bighorn's rock-climbing skills. He and his wife had been following a small herd of bighorn sheep in the mountains of Banff National Park in Canada. They came, as Gildart explained,

> to a point where literally thousands of sheep tracks coursed up and through the rocks. Some followed a straight line, some followed a somewhat sinuous line, while others had absolutely no imaginable pattern at all. What these tracks shared in common was their sure-footed appearance. Elongated skid marks were few, and what few there were remained true to a direct course. Not so with our own tracks, which sometimes skidded and careened wildly.[2]

The bighorns' hooves and structure of their legs are what give them their amazing rock-climbing ability. The hooves are cloven or split. There is a hard outer shell with sharp edges. The center is padded, soft like rubber. The biologist Kim Keating has said that bighorn hooves are like tennis shoes whose skid-proof soles are ringed by a hard core.[3] The structure of the front hooves allows the bighorn to grip small pieces of rock or cling to the smooth surface of steep, sloping rock. This makes it possible for the bighorn to climb slopes that are nearly vertical.

Leaping Sheep

As bighorns zigzag up and down the slopes, they are able to gain a foothold on very narrow ledges, even when the ledge is only 2 inches (5 centimeters) wide. The bighorns' hooves also allow them to land safely after making huge leaps from ledge to ledge, or over steep rocks. Bighorns can jump as much as 20 feet (6 meters) in a single leap. This ability helps bighorns move quickly across rugged territory when fleeing from a predator. Bighorns can run on level ground at speeds up to 30 miles (48 kilometers) per hour. And they can move as fast as 15 miles (24 kilometers) per hour when dashing up a mountain slope. Bighorns spend most of their time close to canyons, cliffs, and other steep places. They prefer such places, which are known as "escape terrain." Bighorns feel safer in such terrain because they can easily run away from predators.

Bighorns also have excellent memories of many details of the landforms in their home range. They know the location of all the cracks,

The structure of bighorns' front hooves enables them to grip small pieces of rock or cling to the smooth surfaces of cliffs, which is how they can climb slopes that are nearly vertical.

crannies, and crevices in the rocky surfaces of the area where they live. When they are running quickly up or down a slope, they do not have to slow down or stop to check their footing. They rely on memory as they dash above or around any obstacles in their path.

Seeing Is Believing

"Bighorns can't hear thunder, can't smell dead horse, but can see through rock."[4] So said an old American Indian guide, as quoted by the naturalist Ernest Thompson Seton, a founding pioneer of the Boy Scouts of America. Of course, the Indian guide was exaggerating. Bighorns actually do have adequate senses of hearing and smell, but their sense of sight is extremely important to these sheep. It allows them to accurately judge distances whenever they jump and need to locate footholds. They also rely on their superb vision to spot distant predators.

Wind currents on the bighorns' high mountain crags are constantly shifting, which lessens the importance of the sense of smell. Also, on high rocky surfaces as well as in desert terrain, the ground is mostly free of branches and twigs. So the sense of hearing would not be of much help in detecting the approach of a predator. However, the bighorns' sense of sight is very important in keeping them safe. A bighorn can usually spot a predator long

▲ *Their keen eyesight allows bighorns like this desert ram to spot predators from a distance.*

before the predator spots him. When a group of bighorns stops to rest, the sheep use a survival strategy that takes full advantage of their excellent eyesight. The sheep lie on the ground at different angles. This way, they can watch for possible predators in every direction.

Several naturalists, including Jack O'Connor, believe that the bighorns' eyesight is as strong as an eight-power set of binoculars (which describes the magnification). O'Connor observed a bighorn watching a coyote. The coyote was so far away that O'Connor could not see it with his naked eye. However, he was able to see the coyote by using an 8 × 30 set of binoculars.[5]

▶ Adaptation to Cold

Bighorn sheep have adapted well to survive in regions of extreme cold and heat. As a result, bighorns are able to live in places where there are not many predators. The mountain-dwelling bighorns' high mountain habitat in winter is an incredibly harsh environment. So is the desert-dwelling bighorns' scorching desert in summer. Winter temperatures in mountain bighorn habitats are usually below freezing (32°F, 0°C), occasionally falling well below zero degrees Fahrenheit during cold snaps. Snowfall is extremely heavy in many of the high-mountain bighorn habitats. A record snowfall of over 93 feet (28 meters) was

▲ *The bodies of mountain bighorns are insulated enough to withstand bitterly cold temperatures. Their short legs expose less surface area to the elements, and their thick shoulders form a heat-conserving block against winds.*

recorded at Mount Rainier in Washington State during the winter of 1971–1972.

One winter day, Bert Gildart and his wife, Jane, were hiking in the mountains of Banff National Park looking for bighorns. Gildart de-scribed a group of bighorns they came across: "Scattered before us were rams, ewes, and lambs, most with crusted snow clinging to their hides and clumping around their eyes. And all around them were depressions in the snow, heralding that they had weathered a frigid night, out in the open in the howling wind."[6] The Gildarts checked the snow from the bighorns' beds. The snow was only slightly crusted. This meant that little heat had escaped from the bighorns' bodies.

▶ Coping in the Cold

In the winter, bighorns do not hibernate. Mountain bighorns' bodies are well insulated to retain heat in cold weather. Their thick shoulders create a blocky form that helps conserve heat. Their short legs reduce the amount of exposed surface area. This lessens heat loss from radia-tion. An outer layer of brittle guard hair protects an under layer of fur or fleece, allowing the bighorns' coats to hold in heat. At high altitudes, the bighorns' heart has to pump harder to com-pensate for lack of oxygen. Because the heart has

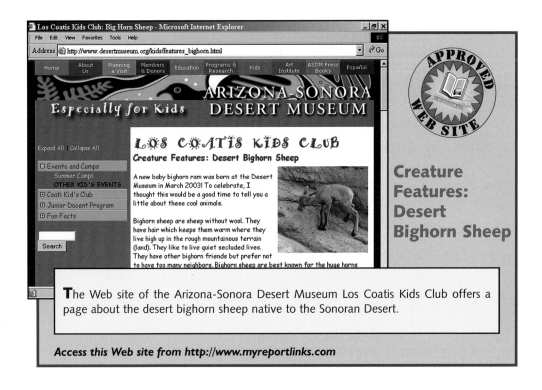

The Web site of the Arizona-Sonora Desert Museum Los Coatis Kids Club offers a page about the desert bighorn sheep native to the Sonoran Desert.

Access this Web site from http://www.myreportlinks.com

to use more energy, the metabolic rate goes up, and the sheep require more food. Their circulatory system nearly shuts down. This also conserves the animals' energy.

To find food in the winter, bighorns try to avoid the deep snows that accumulate at the higher elevations. In the fall, they move downhill to lower elevations, where there is little or no snow and available food, which is why the bighorns spend winter there. In the spring, they move back up to the high elevations. Sometimes, bighorns escape harsh conditions by moving around the mountain, from a north-facing slope to a south-facing slope.

Because there is more sunshine there, the air is warmer and there is less snow on the ground.

▷ Adaptation to Heat

Summer in the dry deserts often brings temperatures above 120°F (49°C). Bighorns deal with the heat of the desert in summer by panting and sweating. A nest of veins in their nose cools down the blood going to the brain, a process known as selective brain cooling. Bighorns also tend to remain inactive during the hottest part of the day. They seek shelter in caves and under overhanging rocks. There they bed down in the shade, sometimes for seven hours or more.

Desert bighorns often cannot find water in summer in the desert. Many water holes are dry, and many creeks and streams are seasonal and go completely dry in the summer months. So when bighorns find a water hole that is not dry, they quickly drink a huge quantity of water. Bighorns can drink as much as one gallon per minute, and up to 7 or more gallons at a time. They can drink up to 20 percent of their body weight at one time. They often have to go from five to fifteen days without drinking until they come to another source of water.

One broiling-hot summer day in Death Valley, California, researchers Florence and Ralph Welles observed two bighorns drinking deeply from springs. The animals had been severely dehydrated, but an amazing transformation occurred as they drank, as Welles and Welles explain.

> I was marveling at how two animals in such poor condition could do this when I suddenly realized that they were no longer in poor condition! The potbellies were gone, the legs were no longer spindly, and the muscles were smooth and rounded beneath the glistening hides of animals in perfect health. This rapid recovery from it [dehydration], this complete rehydration in so short a time seemed little short of miraculous when observed in full context and relatively. It is one of the most significant single observations we have made.[7]

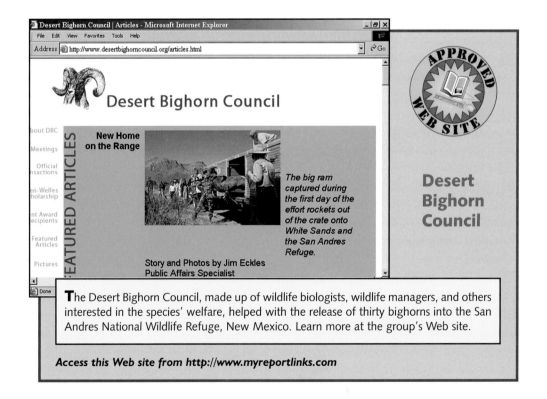

The Desert Bighorn Council, made up of wildlife biologists, wildlife managers, and others interested in the species' welfare, helped with the release of thirty bighorns into the San Andres National Wildlife Refuge, New Mexico. Learn more at the group's Web site.

Access this Web site from http://www.myreportlinks.com

Desert bighorns can get some of the water they need from desert plants. Bighorns in Arizona have been observed eating barrel cactus and saguaro cactus to get the water stored in the plants. The bighorn strikes the cactus plant with his horns to break it open. Then he uses his horns to tear off the plant's outer layer with its sharp spines or needles. The bighorns eat only the inner pulp where the cactus's water is stored.

Each year, bighorns shed their thick winter coat of hair. The hair keeps them warm in the winter, but the bighorns are better off without their coats in the summer. This shedding process, known as "molting," usually takes up to one month, and three months in females who are pregnant or nursing. In the south, molting can begin as early as March. In the north, molting occurs during the summer, usually beginning in May or June. The bighorns' hair, which comes off in mats, looks like towels draping from their bodies. The animals are uncomfortable during this time. They use trees and rocky surfaces as scratching boards to try to speed up the process. By October, the bighorns have grown back a new coat to protect them through the winter.

▶ Something to Chew On

Bighorn sheep are herbivores, which means they eat plants but not animals. Their diet consists of a

Bighorns graze on and off throughout the day to get enough to eat.

surprisingly large variety of plants, considering the harshness of their mountain and desert habitats. In Arizona's Sonoran Desert, scientists have compiled a list of 121 plant species that desert bighorns eat. Scientists studying bighorn sheep in the mountains of British Columbia have drawn up a list of 79 species of plants eaten by the bighorns that live there.[8]

▶ Food for Thought

Bighorns are diurnal. They tend to feed on and off throughout the day and sleep during the night. In the mountains, bighorns feed on browse, grass, and sedges. Browse consist of leaves, shoots, and twigs of shrubs and other woody plants. In summer, the bighorns mostly feed on grasses, including bluegrass, wheatgrass, bromes, and fescues. When grasses are not available, they will eat buds of aspen, spruce, Douglas fir, willow, currant, rose, and juniper. In winter, bighorns feed on the tender shoots of plants such as willow, sage, and rabbit brush. In the dry desert, bighorns feed mostly on brushy plants such as desert holly, desert mallow, and on various types of cactus. Grasses and forbs are also occasionally eaten. Forbs are herbs other than grass.

The large stomachs and complex digestive systems of bighorn sheep and other ruminants, such as goats, cattle, antelope, deer, and giraffes, have

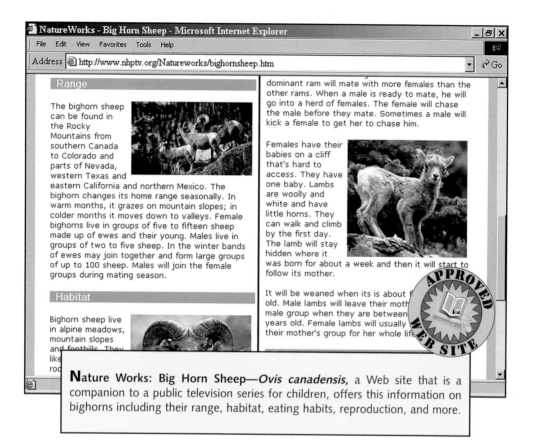

NatureWorks - Big Horn Sheep - Microsoft Internet Explorer

File   Edit   View   Favorites   Tools   Help

Address 🔲 http://www.nhptv.org/Natureworks/bighornsheep.htm

Range

The bighorn sheep can be found in the Rocky Mountains from southern Canada to Colorado and parts of Nevada, western Texas and eastern California and northern Mexico. The bighorn changes its home range seasonally. In warm months, it grazes on mountain slopes; in colder months it moves down to valleys. Female bighorns live in groups of five to fifteen sheep made up of ewes and their young. Males live in groups of two to five sheep. In the winter bands of ewes may join together and form large groups of up to 100 sheep. Males will join the female groups during mating season.

Habitat

Bighorn sheep live in alpine meadows, mountain slopes and foothills. They like ro[...]

dominant ram will mate with more females than the other rams. When a male is ready to mate, he will go into a herd of females. The female will chase the male before they mate. Sometimes a male will kick a female to get her to chase him.

Females have their babies on a cliff that's hard to access. They have one baby. Lambs are woolly and white and have little horns. They can walk and climb by the first day. The lamb will stay hidden where it was born for about a week and then it will start to follow its mother.

It will be weaned when its is about f[...] old. Male lambs will leave their moth[...] male group when they are between [...] years old. Female lambs will usually [...] their mother's group for her whole lif[...]

Nature Works: Big Horn Sheep—*Ovis canadensis,* a Web site that is a companion to a public television series for children, offers this information on bighorns including their range, habitat, eating habits, reproduction, and more.

evolved over time to digest grasses. Ruminants have a four-chambered stomach, made up of a rumen, reticulum, omasum, and abomasum. The digestive process begins when the bighorn quickly bites off and chews leaves, grass, twigs, or other plant parts. By the age of four, bighorns have their permanent teeth. Their incisors and a single canine tooth are used for nipping the food. The molars grind the food. Because the molars get worn down by the coarseness of most of the food bighorns eat, the molars grow throughout the sheep's life.

After first chewing the food, the bighorn swallows it. The bits of vegetation are quickly passed down to the first chamber of the stomach, the rumen. After eating, the bighorn lies down to rest. Then, the bighorn regurgitates the food. The wad of food, called the cud, travels from the bighorn's gullet back into its mouth. After chewing the cud thoroughly, the bighorn swallows it. The food quickly moves through the rumen again. Then it continues on to the three other stomach chambers to complete the digestive process.

This complex digestion is necessary because most plants in the bighorns' diet contain tough cell walls and chemicals that are difficult to digest. The rumen contains bacteria and other microscopic organisms that break down the cell walls and chemicals in the food. The bighorns' rumen is larger than that of other cud chewers. And it is the large rumen that allows the bighorn sheep to live in places that would be uninhabitable for other cud chewers.

BIGHORN BEHAVIOR

Bighorn sheep are social animals that live in groups. Biologists studying them believe that there are several reasons for this. Bighorns in groups stand a better chance of protecting themselves from predators since a predator will more easily be spotted before it has a chance to make a kill. When one of the bighorns in the group spots a predator, the sheep come to attention, standing and staring at the source. If bighorns are threatened by wolves, the sheep will huddle in a tight circle, facing outward. If a predator at close range startles the bighorns, the group will run quickly.

▶ Strength in Numbers

It is also possible that bighorns in groups will have better luck than a lone sheep in finding the best available sources of food. Another benefit of group living is that bighorns can help each other to find good breeding grounds, find mates more easily, and find water sources more readily. Bighorns use their tongue to groom each other's face, ears, or horns. By doing this, the bighorns

Bighorns are social animals, meaning they find strength— and protection—in numbers.

can get rid of ticks or other pests that may cling to their bodies.

▷ Divided by Sex

For most of the year, though, ewes and rams live in separate groups. Adult rams band together in a group called a bachelor herd. Adult ewes form their own "nursery" group, which also consists of lambs and immature rams. Dr. Kathreen Ruckstuhl, a biology professor from the University of Calgary, has studied bighorns in groups and has observed that rams and ewes move in different ways. Ruckstuhl studied the way bighorns walked, grazed, and rested. She noticed that rams spent more time resting than ewes did, and the ewes spent more time walking and feeding than the rams did. Ruckstuhl reasoned that perhaps these different behaviors make it difficult for rams and ewes to travel together easily, which may be why they form separate groups.

Bighorn groups usually consist of five to fifteen individual sheep. Mountain bighorn groups tend to be

▲ *A ewe (right) and her lamb. For most of the year, rams travel in different groups than ewes and lambs do.*

slightly larger than those in the desert. In the most northerly regions, groups of fifty are not uncommon. Perhaps there is a need for larger groups because there is a greater danger from predators in the mountains. Within the bachelor herd, the ram with the largest horns is usually the leader of the group. This ram has established his dominance by winning battles against any challenger.

Within the ewe-lamb group as well, a dominant ewe becomes the leader. Although battles between ewes are not common, they do happen. The ewes' horns are considerably smaller than those of the rams. But ewes can use their horns in combat if necessary. However, a ewe usually gets to lead a herd because of her age and experience. In the fall, during mating season, when the bachelor herds and the ewe-lamb herds come together, the dominant ram usually leads the combined herd. The other rams in the group acknowledge their leader by rubbing their eye glands on him, by licking his horns, and by sniffing him.

▷ Bighorn Communication

Bighorn ewes are usually silent. When a ewe has finished feeding, though, she will call her young with a series of soft "blatts." These sounds are similar to the "baas" of domestic sheep. If a lamb has strayed and does not respond, the ewe calls out loudly. Lambs also call out when it is time to eat.

Bighorn rams, on the other hand, are much more vocal and communicate through a complex system of body language. Rams are most vocal during fights or when a new sheep enters the group. They make a low rumbling sound that is difficult to hear from a distance. Then they may grunt or snort, or gnash or grind their teeth. But starting at a very early age, rams also begin using their horns as a means of communication.

▶ Butting In

Young bighorn rams "horn" each other, pushing and shoving and butting their heads against one another. Even though their horns are not fully developed, the young rams are testing each other. They check each other's strengths and weaknesses to establish their order in the group. The quest for dominance continues throughout the rams' lives.

Scientists have observed several basic types of communication signals used by rams. A common signal, known as the "low stretch," is often used by rams and occasionally by

The quest for dominance among rams continues throughout their lives.

ewes. The bighorn holds its head low to the ground and outstretched. This gesture indicates submissiveness to another sheep of the same sex. For rams, the gesture is also a way to show off their horn size. For extra emphasis, a ram may twist his neck during the display, a gesture known as "the twist."

Rams often like to show how tough they are by using one of their front legs to kick another ram. First, the ram barrels into his opponent with his chest. Then, he usually delivers a series of kicks to the side of his opponent.

Sizing Up Each Other

Bighorn sheep often communicate with one an-other by sniffing each other. Rams often gather together in huddles, with their faces inward and their rumps pointed outward. During these hud-dles, the rams sniff each other. Sometimes, a subordinate ram may chew the horn of a domi-nant ram. Sheep have a suborbital gland located just below the eye. When the rams gather in a huddle, they rub noses against this gland. Secretions from the gland help the rams identify each other and allow subordinates to recognize dominant rams. Knowing "who is who" in the so-cial ranking of the group lessens the possibility of fighting, which could lead to injury.

▲ A pair of mountain rams butt heads in the snows of Wyoming. When rams engage in clashes, they may run at each other at speeds averaging twenty miles per hour.

▶ Clash and Crash

One of the most interesting parts of bighorn behavior comes during the prerut, which is one to two months before rutting, or mating season. At this time, the bighorn rams begin to engage in spectacular head clashes. According to Olaus J. Murie, a renowned field biologist who also served as director of the Wilderness Society, "In the autumn, if you are in mountain sheep country, you may hear a loud whack as if someone had slammed two stout boards together, or had

Two mountain rams size each other up during rutting. This photograph comes from **Animal Field Guide: Bighorn Sheep**, a Web site of the Montana Fish, Wildlife and Parks Department. The site also includes a field guide to the state's bighorn sheep population.

banged shut a car door. Follow the sound, and you may come upon two jealous rams fighting by simply banging their heads together."[1]

Before rams charge at each other, they push and shove each other about. Then they turn away from each other, pretending to graze. Suddenly, both rams turn and face each another. They rear up on their hind legs, drop down, and then charge while lowering their neck. The two rams make a mad dash toward each other at speeds of up to 20 miles (32 kilometers) per hour. Then their foreheads collide with a loud crash that can often be heard from more than a mile away.

▷ Battling Bighorns

Sometimes, a ram with really large horns will intimidate an opponent into backing down before the fight even begins. Many times, the battle will be over after one clash of the horns. But often, rams keep charging each other, butting heads again and again. An observer in California's Death Valley watched as two rams crashed into each other more than forty times in two hours. Sometimes, these head-to-head battles lead to death for one or both of the rams. Such a battle was witnessed by photographer Michael Francis, who recorded the combat between two bighorn sheep along the side of a steep cliff. According to Francis, "They fought for hours, pounding each other until exhausted. Still not satisfied, they continued the battle, locking horns and losing their footing, both plummeting to their deaths on the hard rocks below."[2]

Battles between bighorn rams can occur at anytime during the year, but most of the fights occur during the prerut and rut. The most serious battles involve the rams that are six to nine years old, since their horns are fully grown, with at least a three-quarter curl. Although rams reach sexual maturity at two years of age, these young rams usually do not get to breed. Their horns are small, with only a one-quarter curl. Only the rams with the biggest horns have a chance of winning a fight. Most fights take place between rams that are fairly evenly matched in horn size.

Finding Mates

In the bighorns' most mountainous and northerly ranges, mating season is usually in the fall. The ewes come into estrus at this time, meaning they are ready for mating. This timing allows 170 to 180 days, or about 6 months, for the gestation period, the time in which the ewe carries her lamb until it is born. The lambs will be born in the spring, when food is more plentiful. In the deserts, estrus occurs earlier because food is available for a longer time. Young, socially immature rams actually do sometimes get to breed. These low-ranking rams use a combat tactic known as coursing, which is a kind of free-for-all, against older, much stronger rams. The goal of younger rams is to win a few seconds to mate with a ewe. As foolish as this behavior might seem, the young rams sometimes succeed, but they are more often badly injured or even killed by the dominant ram.

During the fall, the muscular adult rams are well fed and in top shape. They must fight to

▲ A bighorn ewe. Ewes have horns that are more slender and also straighter than the horns rams have.

determine which one will acquire the highest breeding status. The winner earns dominance over the ewes in estrus. The rams move from one group of ewes to another, fighting over those ready to mate, but it is the dominant ram in each group that gets to do most of the breeding. Subordinate rams sometimes get to breed, but this usually depends on a lucky encounter with a ewe when the dominant ram is elsewhere.

A dominant ram and ewe may mate as many as a dozen times or more. One researcher observed a ram and ewe mating thirty-eight times over the course of a couple of hours, although each union lasted only about a minute. After mating with a ewe, the ram moves on and mates with other ewes. Bighorn sheep partners do not establish social relationships. After a ewe gives birth, the ram plays no role in raising the lamb.

▶ Baby Bighorns: Lambs

Mountain bighorn sheep give birth to lambs in late spring. The ewe needs to eat well while she is nursing, and food in the mountains is most plentiful in the spring. Desert bighorns can have lambs during any month of the year. In the Mojave Desert, in California, most lamb births occur during February and March.

Ewes give birth to one lamb. Although extremely rare, twin births have occurred in

This bighorn lamb seems unsure how to take its next step, but it will soon be able to climb as adeptly as its mother. This photograph and others are found on **NatureServe Explorer Bighorn Sheep,** a Web page available through the database of NatureServe, a nonprofit conservation organization.

bighorns. A ewe usually gives birth for the first time at the age of two or three years. It is possible for the ewe to continue to have lambs for the rest of her life. Shortly before she gives birth, the ewe will separate herself from the flock. She then finds a secluded spot that is safe from predators. There she will bed down and give birth. Ewes give birth while lying down.

Bighorn lambs weigh from six to ten pounds (three to five kilograms) at birth. Newborns are covered with hair and show no evidence of horns.

Right after birth, the ewes spend about twenty minutes licking their lambs dry. The ewes then nuzzle the lambs and begin to nurse them. Within just hours of being born, lambs rise to their feet. They stand beneath the ewe's stomach. They stretch their necks so that they can suckle milk from their mother's udder.

A Lamb's First Days and Months

During its first day, the lamb is playful. It moves about, developing its reflexes and strengthening its limbs. Although it can now wander off, it stays

▲ A young bighorn, its horns just beginning to show, perches on the side of a rocky cliff. Jumping from one treacherous spot to another is one of the most important skills a young bighorn must learn if it is to survive.

close to its mother, following her about. Within several days of the birth, the ewe rejoins the herd. She now seeks the added safety of being part of the group. The ewe-lamb bands situate themselves in locations where they can easily spot predators. The ewes may take turns guarding while the others feed, or each ewe may have to fend for herself.

Meanwhile, the frisky young lamb continues its playful behavior. Belonging to the ewe-lamb herd gives it the opportunity to learn to interact with other lambs. Within four weeks, the young lamb looks like one of its parents but without the horns.

During their first several months, lambs begin to jump from one treacherous rock to another. This is probably the most important skill the bighorn lamb must gain to survive, and it is a skill not easily learned. Sadly, miscalculated leaps can and do lead to the lamb's death.

Within four to six months after giving birth, ewes wean their lambs. They do this by just walking away from the lambs quickly after allowing them to nurse for a few seconds. By the age of six months, lambs are almost as tall as their mothers and weigh about eighty pounds (forty kilograms). At this age, male and female lambs have horns, so the butting begins! They begin to butt each other and also have a go at trees and rocks.

Chapter 5

HISTORY OF BIGHORN-HUMAN CONTACT

About one million years ago, bighorn sheep began migrating from Asia to North America. They crossed the land bridge connecting what are now Siberia and Alaska. Much later, possibly as early as thirty-five thousand years ago during a more recent ice age, the first human beings arrived in North America. They, too, crossed the land bridge from Siberia to Alaska. These first people in North America were nomadic hunters, who followed herds of wild animals that provided them with food, clothing, and materials for shelter. For the first time in North America, bighorn sheep faced a dangerous new predator—the human being.

▶ Bighorn Sheep and American Indians

Bighorn sheep were more important to the ancestors of American Indians than any other animal. Evidence of their importance exists throughout the western United States, especially in the Southwest. Thousands of pictographs and petroglyphs depicting bighorn sheep can be found

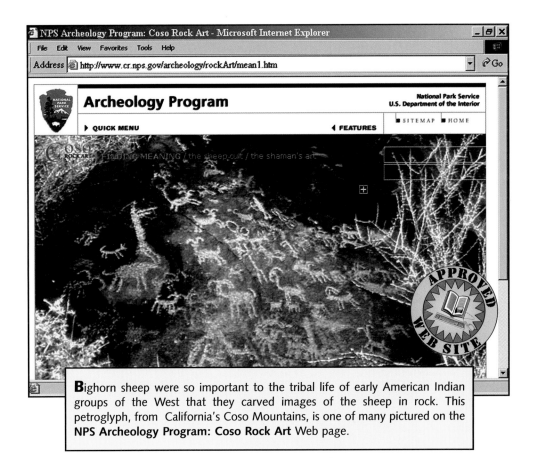

Bighorn sheep were so important to the tribal life of early American Indian groups of the West that they carved images of the sheep in rock. This petroglyph, from California's Coso Mountains, is one of many pictured on the **NPS Archeology Program: Coso Rock Art** Web page.

on remote canyon walls, cliffs, and the rock walls inside caves. Pictographs are paintings on rock, while petroglyphs are carvings in rock. The oldest petroglyphs are at least three thousand years old. Pictographs date from about A.D. 500.

One morning, writer Bert Gildart was wandering in a canyon high up in the Coso Mountains of California. As the sun rose, Gildart stared in amazement as the sunlight revealed ancient inscriptions on the canyon wall. He wrote,

"Deeper now in the canyon I could see images of bows and arrows, shaman and deer, but it was sheep that dominated. There were square-bodied sheep, round-bodied sheep, inverted sheep, erect sheep, large-horned sheep, sheep inside other sheep."[1]

▶ Sheep in Art

In 1980, Campbell Grant, a scientist, did a survey of sites featuring bighorn sheep rock art. He found that the site with the greatest concentration of such rock art is in the Coso Range of southern

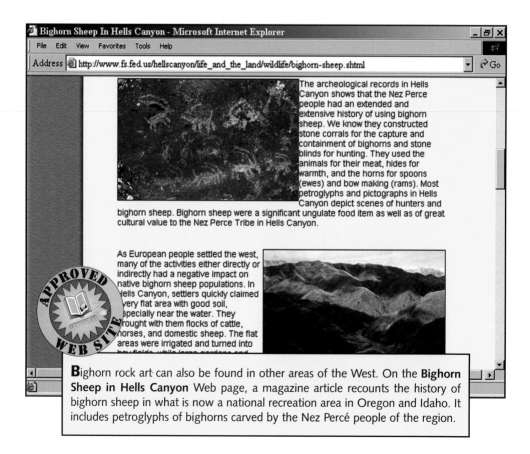

Bighorn Sheep In Hells Canyon - Microsoft Internet Explorer

File   Edit   View   Favorites   Tools   Help

Address http://www.fs.fed.us/hellscanyon/life_and_the_land/wildlife/bighorn-sheep.shtml   Go

The archeological records in Hells Canyon shows that the Nez Perce people had an extended and extensive history of using bighorn sheep. We know they constructed stone corrals for the capture and containment of bighorns and stone blinds for hunting. They used the animals for their meat, hides for warmth, and the horns for spoons (ewes) and bow making (rams). Most petroglyphs and pictographs in Hells Canyon depict scenes of hunters and bighorn sheep. Bighorn sheep were a significant ungulate food item as well as of great cultural value to the Nez Perce Tribe in Hells Canyon.

As European people settled the west, many of the activities either directly or indirectly had a negative impact on native bighorn sheep populations. In Hells Canyon, settlers quickly claimed very flat area with good soil, especially near the water. They brought with them flocks of cattle, horses, and domestic sheep. The flat areas were irrigated and turned into

Bighorn rock art can also be found in other areas of the West. On the **Bighorn Sheep in Hells Canyon** Web page, a magazine article recounts the history of bighorn sheep in what is now a national recreation area in Oregon and Idaho. It includes petroglyphs of bighorns carved by the Nez Percé people of the region.

California. More than half of the one hundred thousand petroglyphs there depict bighorn sheep. Other important sites include the Four Corners area (the point where Colorado, New Mexico, Arizona, and Utah meet), south-central Oregon, and the Columbia River Gorge along the Washington-Oregon border.

Many scientists believe the ancient rock art's purpose was to convey certain messages. The images of bighorn sheep, at least in some cases, were probably meant as hunting "magic." They were created to ensure good luck on the hunt. The petroglyphs often depict bighorns as the quarry of the hunt. Some of the earliest petroglyphs included carvings of people hurling an atlatl. The atlatl was a throwing stick with a spearhead attached to it, used for hunting. Then, about two thousand years ago, American Indians began using a bow and arrow. Petroglyphs from that time on sometimes show people hunting bighorns with those weapons.

Sheep as Spiritual Guides

Archaeologist David Whitely has a different theory about the purpose of bighorn rock art images. He believes the images were created by shamans, or medicine men, who were seeking rain during severe droughts. The shamans believed that the supernatural world was the opposite of the earthly

http://www.petroglyphs.us/IC-22_bighorn_sheep_petroglyphs.jpg - Microsoft Internet Explorer

File   Edit   View   Favorites   Tools   Help

Address http://www.petroglyphs.us/IC-22_bighorn_sheep_petroglyphs.jpg   Go

Done

Images of bighorns adorn the rock walls of a canyon found on the north side of Black Mountain, near Barstow, California, where Paiute and Shoshone people were once active. This photograph and other photos of rock art come from the **Inscription Canyon Rock Art Petroglyphs** Web page.

world. In other words, if one wanted help from the spirits in making rain, then one had to contact the spirits in the driest spots.[2] The driest locations happened to be the habitat of bighorn sheep. The shamans believed the bighorn to be the spiritual guide of rainmaking. The canyons of the American Southwest were the openings into the supernatural home of the bighorn spirit guide.

Much of the rock art in the Southwest is the work of the Ancient Pueblo people or Anasazi, a prehistoric American Indian people who lived in

Arizona, New Mexico, and southwestern Colorado. Later peoples, including the Hopi, Navajo, Acoma, and Papago, among others, had their own bighorn sheep deities. The Papago of southern California took the horns of bighorn sheep killed by their hunters and piled them together near water holes. They believed that this would allow them to control the wind and prevent the air from leaving the earth.

First Sightings of Bighorns by Europeans

In 1540, the Spanish explorer Francisco Vásquez de Coronado led an expedition through what is now the southwestern United States. In a report to the governor of Mexico, he mentioned that he had encountered " . . . some sheep as big as a horse, with very large horns."[3] Coronado was clearly impressed by bighorn sheep, even if he slightly exaggerated their size.

In the years that followed, other European explorers and missionaries spotted bighorn sheep in northwestern Mexico and the American Southwest. In 1697, Father Francisco Maria Piccolo, a Jesuit priest, published an account of the bighorn in which he wrote, "Its Head is much like that of a stag: and its horns, which are very large, like those of a Ram; Its Tail and Hair are speckled, and shorter than a Stags; But its Hoof is large, round, and cleft as an Oxes."[4]

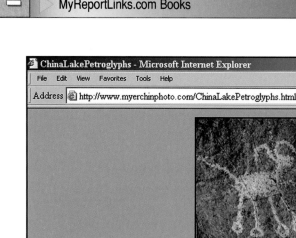

ChinaLakePetroglyphs - Microsoft Internet Explorer

File   Edit   View   Favorites   Tools   Help

Address http://www.myerchinphoto.com/ChinaLakePetroglyphs.html   Go

The most common petroglyph in the Cosos is the Bighorn Sheep.
Vision of bighorn sheep spirits were believed to yield rainmaking
power because Bighorns were the special spirit helpers of Rain-
shaman. The large numbers of bighorn petroglyphs in the Cosos
reflect the belief that it was the best location throughout the Numic
speaking region to obtain rainmaking power. Historical accounts
indicate that shamans came from as far as northeastern Utah to the

Done

The bighorn sheep is the most common petroglyph carved into the walls of the
Coso Mountains of California. Ancient tribes revered the sheep as a helper to
spiritual leaders known as shaman, whom they believed to have magical
powers. This image comes from the **China Lake Petroglyphs** Web page.

In 1757, an illustration of a bighorn sheep
appeared in a book for the first time. The book,
A Natural and Civil History of California (first
printed in Spanish, then in English four years later),
referred to the bighorn as the "California deer." In
1803, George Shaw, a zoologist with the British
Museum in London, England, examined the re-
mains of a bighorn sheep that had been sent to him
from the United States. He became the first person
to take measurements and describe features of
the bighorn sheep in a scientific way.[5]

▶ Lewis and Clark's Encounters

In 1804, Meriwether Lewis and William Clark were sent by President Thomas Jefferson to explore the lands west of the Missouri River all the way to the Pacific coast. On May 25, 1805, the members of the Lewis and Clark expedition were camped along the upper Missouri River, near what is now the border of Montana and North Dakota. That day, they encountered bighorn sheep for the first time. William Clark killed a bighorn ewe. His interpreter of Indian languages, George Drewyer, killed a bighorn ram, and another member of the expedition, William Bratten, later killed another ewe.

Lewis described the bighorns he encountered and their usefulness to the American Indians of the area. Clark copied Lewis's description into his journal:

> It [the male] was somewhat larger than the mail [male] of the Common Deer; the body reather thicker deeper and not so long in proportion to it's hight as the common Deer; the head and horns of the male are remarkably large compared with the other parts of the animal . . . the horn is of a light brown colour; when dressed it is almost white extreamly transparent and very elastic. This horn is used by the natives in constructing their bows; I have no doubt of it's elegance and usefullness in hair combs, and might possibly answer as maney valuable purpoces to civilized man, as it does to the native indians, who form their water cups, spoons, and platters of it.[6]

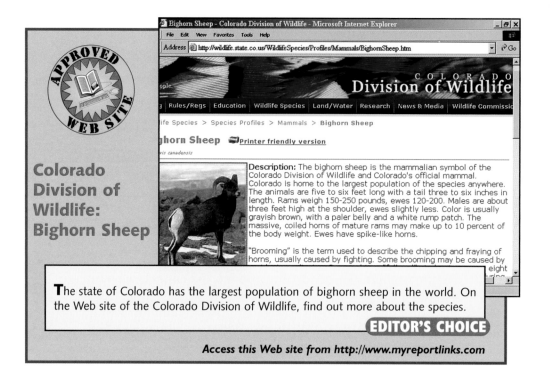

Colorado
Division of
Wildlife:
Bighorn Sheep

The state of Colorado has the largest population of bighorn sheep in the world. On the Web site of the Colorado Division of Wildlife, find out more about the species.

EDITOR'S CHOICE

Access this Web site from http://www.myreportlinks.com

William Clark and other early explorers of the West believed that bighorn sheep would not be a good source of meat to feed the members of their expeditions. The sheep were too difficult to get to, and they were not large enough to be worth the trouble it took to hunt them. So most trappers and explorers at the time did not bother much with bighorn sheep, preferring to hunt bison. Clark described their difficulty in reaching the sheep.

> They feed on grass, but principally on the arra-matic herbs which grows on the clifts and inaxcessable hights which they frequent most commonly, and the places they generally collect to lodge is the crannies of crevices of the rocks in the face of inaxcessable precepices, where the

wolf nor Bear can reach them, and where indeed man himself would in maney instances find a similar deficiency . . . they are very shy and quick of both sent [scent] and sight.[7]

▶ Other Sheep Tales

In 1823, Alexander Ross was exploring the Blue Mountains in Oregon for the North West Company, which traded in furs. One day, he came across the skull of a bighorn sheep embedded in a tree trunk. The horns were still attached to it. Ross reported an Indian legend regarding the bighorn skull in the tree.

> Our Flathead Indians related to us a rather strange story about the ram's head. Indian legend relates that as the first Flathead Indians passed this way one of them attacked a mountain ram as large and stout as a common horse, that on wounding him, the fierce animal turned round upon his pursuer, who taking shelter behind the tree, the ram came against it with all his force, so that he drove his head through it, but before he could get it extracted again the Indian killed him and took off the body but left the head, as a memento of the adventure. All Indians reverence the celebrated tree, which they say by the circumstances related conferred on them the power of mastering and killing all animals.[8]

Although most explorers and trappers considered the hunting of bighorn sheep to be dangerous and a waste of time, there were exceptions. One of the first Americans to appreciate the challenge of

Address http://www.nps.gov/romo/naturescience/big_horn_sheep.htm

nps.gov
(home)

National Park Service
U.S. Department of the Interior

Rocky Mountain

National Park

search   go
◉ Search this park
○ Search nps.gov

text size: A A A

printer friendly

PARK HOME
PLAN YOUR VISIT
PHOTOS & MULTIMEDIA
HISTORY & CULTURE
NATURE & SCIENCE
  Animals
  Birds
  Fish
  Mammals
  Elk
  ▸ Bighorn Sheep
  Amphibians and
  Reptiles

Big Horn Sheep

The recent history of bighorn sheep in Rocky Mountain National Park is a dramatic story of near extinction and encouraging recovery. In the mid-1800's, the population of bighorn in the area numbered in the thousands. As hunters and settlers moved into Estes Valley in the late 1800's and early 1900's, the bighorn population declined rapidly. Initially, market hunters, encouraged by the high prices paid for then prized horns and meat, shot bighorn by the hundreds. When ranchers moved into

NPS PHOTO

Rocky Mountain National Park: Bighorn Sheep

Bighorn sheep were nearly extinct in Rocky Mountain National Park. This National Park Service Web site outlines their return, their dramatic recovery, and their relationship with park patrons.

EDITOR'S CHOICE

Access this Web site from http://www.myreportlinks.com

hunting bighorns was Osborne Russell, a trapper who spent nine years in the Rocky Mountains. In *Journal of a Trapper,* he wrote about how much he enjoyed hiking in the mountains to observe and hunt bighorn sheep. In February 1839, Russell was hunting bighorns near what is now the Idaho-Wyoming border. He described how dangerous his pursuit of bighorns was.

> I have often passed over places where I have had to cut steps in the ice with my butcher Knife to place my feet in directly over the most frightful precipices, but being excited in the pursuit of game I would think little of danger until I had laid down to sleep at night, then it would make my blood run cold to meditate upon the scenes

▲ Big-game "trophies" including bears, bighorns, and elk, were considered valuable enough in the early twentieth century to be part of a White House collection. In this photograph from 1923, George Marshall, a taxidermist with the National Museum, surveys some animal heads from the collection that required his attention.

I had passed thro. [through] during the day and often have I resolved never to risk myself again in such places and as often broken the resolution.[9]

Later, many more hunters would come to regard bighorn sheep as a trophy worth pursuing. The challenge of hunting bighorns became irresistible.

THREATS TO THE SHEEP'S SURVIVAL

During the first half of the nineteenth century, explorers and trappers in the American West reported that bighorn sheep were plentiful and common in many areas. For the most part, though, they were not interested in hunting the sheep. During the second half of that century, however, things changed dramatically when the Southwest was settled by the eastern Americans.

Pioneer settlers hunted large game, including bighorn sheep, to feed their families. Since there were no laws restricting hunting in most places, there was no limit to the number of bighorns that could be killed. Hunting was not the only threat to the bighorn, however. Many settlers brought herds of domestic cattle and sheep with them. As the settlers established farms and ranches, their herds grazed on lands that had once been the home of wild bighorn sheep.

Ever since, humans and their activities have increasingly taken over what was once bighorn habitat. The introduction of domestic animals and the diseases they brought with them contributed

The pioneers who settled the American West in the nineteenth century were the first to affect the region's bighorn population by introducing livestock. The actions of humans are still a threat to the species.

to the decline of the bighorns. Hunting, habitat loss, and disease all threaten the bighorn sheep's survival.

Hunting Bighorns

During the last half of the nineteenth century, bighorn sheep populations in the western United States were greatly affected by human settlement. Hunting was one of the main activities threatening the species. Conservationists were becoming concerned. They began to pressure state legislatures to make laws prohibiting hunting of bighorns.

In 1873, California banned the hunting of bighorns. Other states came up with a two-stage process to regulate the hunting of these sheep. The first stage allowed bighorns to be shot, but only during certain months of the year—an open season. The second stage completely stopped bighorn hunting. In 1895, Nevada passed a law banning the hunting of bighorns except for the period from September 1 to December 31. Even when this law went into effect, the numbers of bighorns continued to fall. So in 1917, Nevada enacted a law totally banning bighorn hunting. Other western states passed similar laws.

Population Swings

With hunting bans in place, bighorns had a chance to recover, and their populations increased. By the

1950s, many wildlife officials believed that the numbers of bighorn sheep had grown enough to allow hunting again. As states dropped the laws banning hunting, the bighorns' numbers began to dwindle once more. Eventually, the various states enacted laws strictly regulating the hunting of bighorns. Open season, usually lasting from November to December, is short. The number of licenses issued to hunt bighorns is limited by law. People caught breaking the laws regarding bighorn hunting are prosecuted.

▲ A herd of so-called "trophy" bighorn. Some early settlers killed bighorns to put meat on their tables, but others killed the large wild sheep as sport—and continue to do so.

Back in the days of the settlement of the West, people mainly hunted bighorns to put meat on the table. But some hunters pursued bighorn rams as trophies, so they could mount the ram's head on a wall. In more recent times, most hunters of bighorns were after such trophies. Hunting for trophy animals threatens the survival of particular bighorn groups because it removes the dominant breeding rams.

To limit the number of rams killed, states set up lottery systems. Sportsmen had to win a license to hunt bighorn rams in a random drawing. The odds were heavily stacked against any individual winning the lottery. The Foundation for North American Wild Sheep holds auctions in which sportsmen bid on permits to hunt bighorn rams. Because the availability of licenses and permits is limited, relatively few bighorns are killed legally each year.

▶ Illegal Hunting

Unfortunately, bighorns are also killed illegally, by poachers who operate outside the law. These people do not care that bighorns are an endangered species, and in their disregard they represent a significant threat to the sheep. There are three types of poachers. The one doing the most damage is the "professional" poacher. The professional hunts bighorns, mainly adult rams, for money.

During the 1930s, posters for the National Park Service championed the bighorn sheep to advertise the service's dedication to preserving wildlife. This poster was part of the Work Projects Administration's Federal Art Project, one of the WPA's Depression-era government programs that employed people in jobs for the public good.

He sells the meat, hide, and horns, and often makes a lot of money doing so: A successful poacher can get more than ten thousand dollars for the mounted head of a bighorn ram.

Some poachers hunt bighorns just to see if they can get away with it. These game-playing poachers seem to think it is fun to try and outwit the game wardens. A third type of poacher is a hunter who kills a bighorn because he or she is unaware of its endangered and protected status. Whatever the poacher's motivation, illegal killing of bighorns is a risky business. Those who are caught may have to pay hefty fines or even serve time in prison.

▶ Nonhuman Hunters of Bighorns

Nonhuman hunters are also a threat to bighorn sheep. In various places, bighorns have been killed by coyotes, wolves, bears, bobcats, and lynx. Golden eagles have been known to swoop down and attack young bighorns wherever they find unprotected lambs. But chief among these natural predators are mountain lions, large wild cats also known as cougars.

In recent years, legislation was passed in many western states that reclassified mountain lions as game animals, which meant that they could no longer be hunted at random. Protected at least part of the year from hunters, mountain lion populations increased. In 1972, mountain lions were given full protection in California. Although no exact population figures exist, it is thought that over the next twenty-five years, the number of mountain lions in the state increased from about twenty-four hundred to six thousand.

Mountain lions are a major threat to both mountain and desert bighorn sheep. In southern California in 1992, scientists placed radio collars on 113 desert bighorns. They monitored the tagged sheep for the next six years. By the end of that period, sixty-one of the bighorns had died.

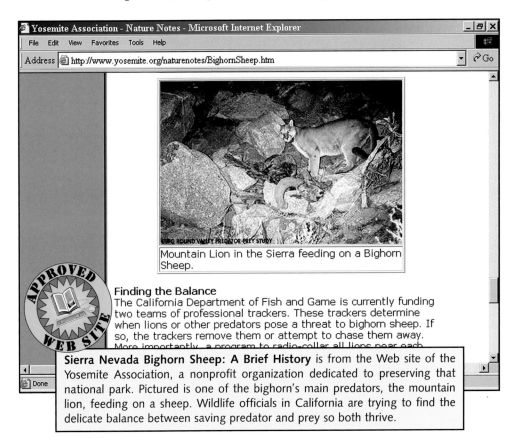

Yosemite Association - Nature Notes - Microsoft Internet Explorer

File Edit View Favorites Tools Help

Address http://www.yosemite.org/naturenotes/BighornSheep.htm

Mountain Lion in the Sierra feeding on a Bighorn Sheep.

Finding the Balance
The California Department of Fish and Game is currently funding two teams of professional trackers. These trackers determine when lions or other predators pose a threat to bighorn sheep. If so, the trackers remove them or attempt to chase them away. More importantly, a program to radio-collar all lions near each

Sierra Nevada Bighorn Sheep: A Brief History is from the Web site of the Yosemite Association, a nonprofit organization dedicated to preserving that national park. Pictured is one of the bighorn's main predators, the mountain lion, feeding on a sheep. Wildlife officials in California are trying to find the delicate balance between saving predator and prey so both thrive.

Forty-two of the bighorns, or 69 percent of the group, were killed by mountain lions. Another dramatic example of the effects of mountain lion predation involves a herd of bighorns in New Mexico. Within an eighteen-month period, the herd of twenty-five bighorns was reduced to a single lone survivor.

Coyotes are another major threat to bighorn sheep, although coyotes mainly kill young lambs. In the spring of 1984 in the National Bison Range in Montana, twenty-three lambs were born in a herd of about fifty bighorns. By mid-September of that year, only two of the lambs were still alive. Most of the other lambs had been killed by coyotes, and more than two thirds had been killed within three days of their birth.

▶ Other Threats: The Spread of Disease

With the settlement of the American West, bighorn sheep had to compete with domestic sheep and cattle for food. Domestic herds also affected the bighorns in another way. Domestic sheep often carry bacteria and viruses that are extremely harmful to wild bighorns. One of the main diseases that bighorns catch from domestic sheep is pneumonia, caused by *Pasteurella,* a bacterium. While domestic sheep can carry these microorganisms without getting sick, bighorn sheep have no resistance to them.

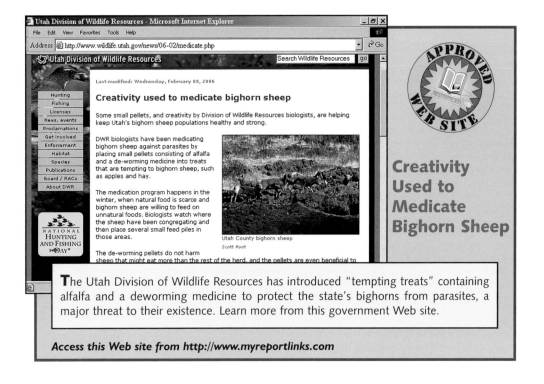

Utah Division of Wildlife Resources - Microsoft Internet Explorer

File   Edit   View   Favorites   Tools   Help

Address http://www.wildlife.utah.gov/news/06-02/medicate.php   Go

Utah Division of Wildlife Resources   Search Wildlife Resources   go

Hunting
Fishing
Licenses
News, events
Proclamations
Get involved
Enforcement
Habitat
Species
Publications
Board / RACs
About DWR

NATIONAL
HUNTING
AND FISHING
DAY®

Last modified: Wednesday, February 08, 2006

Creativity used to medicate bighorn sheep

Some small pellets, and creativity by Division of Wildlife Resources biologists, are helping keep Utah's bighorn sheep populations healthy and strong.

DWR biologists have been medicating bighorn sheep against parasites by placing small pellets consisting of alfalfa and a de-worming medicine into treats that are tempting to bighorn sheep, such as apples and hay.

The medication program happens in the winter, when natural food is scarce and bighorn sheep are willing to feed on unnatural foods. Biologists watch where the sheep have been congregating and then place several small feed piles in those areas.

Utah County bighorn sheep
Scott Root

The de-worming pellets do not harm sheep that might eat more than the rest of the herd, and the pellets are even beneficial to

Creativity Used to Medicate Bighorn Sheep

The Utah Division of Wildlife Resources has introduced "tempting treats" containing alfalfa and a deworming medicine to protect the state's bighorns from parasites, a major threat to their existence. Learn more from this government Web site.

Access this Web site from http://www.myreportlinks.com

In 1989, William J. Foreyt published a study of six healthy bighorns that had been placed in a pen with six domestic sheep. The domestic sheep all appeared healthy, although four of them had *Pasteurella* in their respiratory systems. Within seventy-one days, all of the bighorns had died of pneumonia. The article warned of the danger of bighorns coming into close contact with domestic sheep. According to Foreyt, "On the basis of [the] results of this study and of other reports, domestic sheep and bighorn sheep should not be managed in proximity of each other because of the potential fatal consequences in bighorn sheep."[1]

▷ The Parasite Problem

Bighorns are more vulnerable to pneumonia if they have also become infested with lungworm, a parasite. Parasites are organisms that live on or in another organism and grow and feed on it but do not benefit it. The life cycle of the lungworm requires that it infest two different species of animals, known as the hosts. The lungworm needs a snail and a bighorn sheep to complete its ninety-day life cycle.

During the first stage, the female lungworm lays eggs in the bighorn's lungs. The larvae crawl up into the sheep's mouth and are swallowed. The lungworms are then digested and passed out in feces. During the second stage, snails crawl through the sheep's feces and are penetrated by lungworms. During the third stage, the lungworm larvae develop inside the snails. Then during the fourth stage, the bighorns graze and accidentally eat the snails. The lungworms crawl from the bighorn's stomach to the lungs. The cycle is complete and starts all over again when the lungworms lay eggs in the sheep's lungs.

Almost all sheep have lungworms, and healthy adult bighorns can tolerate lungworm infestations, but baby bighorns cannot. A lamb's immune system is not as developed as an adult sheep's, so lambs can more easily catch pneumonia. In some populations of bighorns, lambs may have more

▲ *Although robust looking, bighorns like this ram are subject to parasitic infections that have drastically reduced certain populations.*

than 30 million lungworm larvae. These lambs cannot survive. Lungworm-pneumonia epizootics (an epizootic is an epidemic among animals) have drastically reduced the population of bighorns in certain places. One such group lived near Pikes Peak in Colorado. In 1970, the herd numbered 1,000. Five years later, after it was affected by a lungworm-pneumonia epizootic, there were only 162 bighorns left. Some biologists today, however, question whether there is a direct link between lungworms and pneumonia.

▶ Other Health Concerns

Other diseases take a heavy toll on bighorn sheep. A parasite known as the nasal botfly causes sinusitis in bighorns, which can kill the sheep. Bighorns in the desert are more likely to suffer from sinusitis, because botflies thrive in dry areas. Another parasite, a scabies mite, infests the ears of bighorns. The loss of hearing from scabies mites could make a bighorn more vulnerable to predators. Scabies mites can also cause infection. A severe scabies epizootic occurred in the San Andres National Wildlife Refuge of New Mexico in 1979. More than 90 percent of the park's bighorns died as a result.

As the West became settled, and bighorn habitat was greatly reduced, the sheep populations became concentrated in smaller areas. This

▲ *If desert bighorns and other bighorn sheep are to survive, threats from epizootics will need to be addressed. Such epidemics have come close to killing entire populations of bighorns.*

A desert bighorn surveys the rocky landscape of its habitat. Efforts to increase desert bighorn populations have met with success in some places. In 2007, in the San Andres National Wildlife Refuge in New Mexico, the park's bighorn population stood at around one hundred, thanks to salvage and treatment programs and continued careful monitoring by wildlife officials and scientists.

increased the likelihood that epizootics would be more severe whenever they struck. According to scientist Francis Singer, "The single greatest obstacle to the restoration of large, healthy populations of bighorn sheep in the western United States is epizootic outbreaks . . . that may kill 20–100% of the animals in populations."[2]

CURRENT EFFORTS TO PROTECT BIGHORN SHEEP

In light of all these threats to bighorns, scientists, conservationists, wildlife officials, and volunteers concerned about the sheep are working to ensure that the species survives. There are now ongoing federal and state programs to manage bighorn herds. Their combined efforts work to control predators wherever possible, monitor different herds, track individual sheep, transplant bighorns, preserve and restore bighorn habitat, repopulate former bighorn habitats, breed captive bighorns, and educate the public about bighorn sheep.

▶ Controlling Predators

In recent years, scientists in various places have kept track of bighorns by placing radio collars around their necks. The process of monitoring signals from the radio transmitter around the sheep's neck is known as radiotelemetry. Monitoring the radio collars enables scientists to track the bighorn's movements. A period of time that goes by with no change in the signals alerts the scientist that something has happened. The

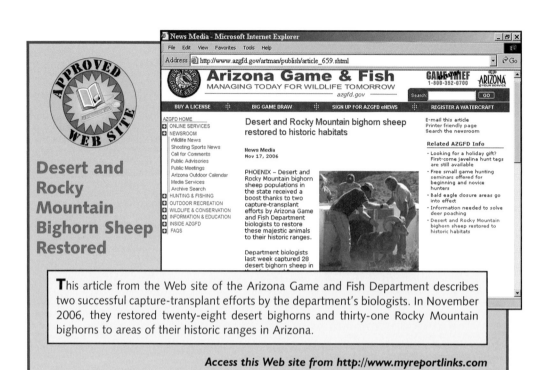

Desert and
Rocky
Mountain
Bighorn Sheep
Restored

This article from the Web site of the Arizona Game and Fish Department describes two successful capture-transplant efforts by the department's biologists. In November 2006, they restored twenty-eight desert bighorns and thirty-one Rocky Mountain bighorns to areas of their historic ranges in Arizona.

Access this Web site from http://www.myreportlinks.com

transmitter may have fallen off the bighorn, or the animal may have died, perhaps killed by a predator. Since the radio signal gives the scientist the animal's location, he or she can find the bighorn and learn what has happened.

Efforts to stabilize or increase the size of bighorn herds by controlling predators have some-times been controversial. The Arizona Game and Fish Department in 2001 came up with a plan to increase the number of bighorn sheep in the Tonto National Forest, near Phoenix. The plan proposed killing about a dozen mountain lions that had been preying on bighorns in the area.

The Arizona Desert Bighorn Sheep Society was in favor of the plan. Gary Barcom, vice president of that organization, said, "It will have a short-term negative impact on the lions, but a long-term positive impact on the sheep and the lions. As unpleasant as that type of management may seem, it's something necessary to bring the two into balance so they can coexist."[1] The Sierra Club disagreed. According to Sandy Bahr, the club's Arizona conservation chairperson, "They'd be killing off the mountain lions for no reason. Predators and prey have evolved over thousands of years. Just because you get rid of the predator doesn't mean you'll improve the population of the prey."[2]

▷ Counting—and Then Moving—Sheep

Scientists need to know the size of a bighorn herd before they can make appropriate recovery plans for it. They not only need to know how many sheep there are in total but also how many rams and ewes there are. A census can be taken from the air by a series of helicopter flights. In desert regions, scientists can count the number of sheep that gather to drink at water holes.

Transplanting, or translocating, bighorn sheep from one area to another is an effective way of increasing the size of a herd. A larger herd size increases the chances of the group's survival. The new additions to the herd help

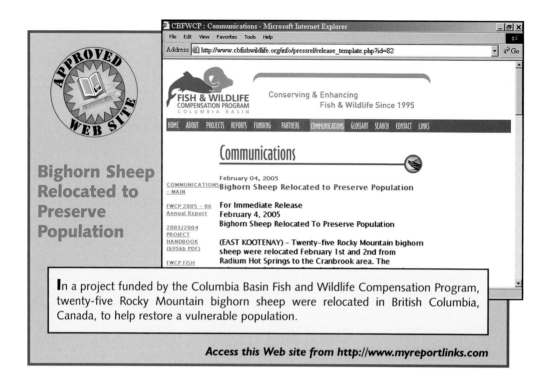

Bighorn Sheep
Relocated to
Preserve
Population

CBFWCP : Communications - Microsoft Internet Explorer

File   Edit   View   Favorites   Tools   Help

Address http://www.cbfishwildlife.org/info/pressrel/release_template.php?id=82   Go

FISH & WILDLIFE
COMPENSATION PROGRAM
C O L U M B I A   B A S I N

Conserving & Enhancing
Fish & Wildlife Since 1995

HOME   ABOUT   PROJECTS   REPORTS   FUNDING   PARTNERS   COMMUNICATIONS   GLOSSARY   SEARCH   CONTACT   LINKS

Communications

February 04, 2005
COMMUNICATIONS Bighorn Sheep Relocated to Preserve Population
– MAIN

FWCP 2005 – 06   **For Immediate Release**
Annual Report   **February 4, 2005**
2003/2004   **Bighorn Sheep Relocated To Preserve Population**
PROJECT
HANDBOOK   (EAST KOOTENAY) – Twenty-five Rocky Mountain bighorn
(695kb PDF)   sheep were relocated February 1st and 2nd from
FWCP FISH   Radium Hot Springs to the Cranbrook area. The

In a project funded by the Columbia Basin Fish and Wildlife Compensation Program, twenty-five Rocky Mountain bighorn sheep were relocated in British Columbia, Canada, to help restore a vulnerable population.

Access this Web site from http://www.myreportlinks.com

make the gene pool more diverse, lessening the chances of inbreeding and health problems caused by it. Sometimes, entire herds have been transplanted. As a result, places where bighorns once roamed but where the herds had become extinct—such as the Black Hills of South Dakota and parts of North Dakota and Texas—are once again home to the sheep.

▷ Mapping Before Capturing

Before a transplantation occurs, scientists thoroughly research the geography of the proposed new home range for the transplanted bighorns. The scientists use computer programs known as geographic information systems (GIS). A GIS program provides a sophisticated mapping system. All the information about a geographic area relevant to the needs of bighorn sheep is included in the GIS program. Specific data about potential hazards in the area is also included. By using GIS programs, scientists are able to determine whether or not a proposed transplantation makes sense, which helps ensure the success of a transplantation when it happens.

To transplant a bighorn, the animal first needs to be captured. Several methods have been used. With a net-gun, a small explosive charge sends the net over the heads of the bighorns. With a

This Web page from the San Diego Zoo is filled with information about sheep. It includes videos and sound bites as well as information about how to distinguish between sheep and goats.

Access this Web site from http://www.myreportlinks.com

drop-net, a net can also be dropped over the heads of the bighorns from a tall structure. With a drive-net, the bighorns are herded into stationary nets. Another method involves shooting a dart containing a tranquilizer into the bighorn. According to veterinarians, this method is the most stressful for the animal and should not be used unless absolutely necessary.

Restoring Bighorn Habitats

Restoring the habitat of bighorns often involves managing the vegetation of the area. The tamarisk, or salt cedar, is a nonnative plant that grows in certain bighorn habitats in the deserts of the Southwest. The tamarisk tends to displace native vegetation that the bighorn feeds on. It also uses up a lot of water. Tamarisks growing near water holes used by bighorns can absorb all of the water, leaving nothing for the sheep. Conservationists are making efforts in many places to get rid of the tamarisks.

Another problem in bighorn habitats occurs when forests grow so thick that bighorns can no longer follow their old familiar trails. Conservationists carry out controlled burns, burning certain areas of land under controlled conditions, to maintain a balanced environment. Fire opens up the forest floor, the vegetation closest to the ground. The bighorn sheep can then once again use their

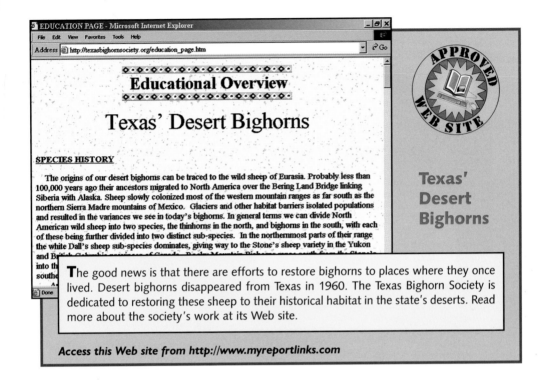

EDUCATION PAGE - Microsoft Internet Explorer

File   Edit   View   Favorites   Tools   Help

Address http://texasbighornsociety.org/education_page.htm   Go

Educational Overview

Texas' Desert Bighorns

SPECIES HISTORY

The origins of our desert bighorns can be traced to the wild sheep of Eurasia. Probably less than 100,000 years ago their ancestors migrated to North America over the Bering Land Bridge linking Siberia with Alaska. Sheep slowly colonized most of the western mountain ranges as far south as the northern Sierra Madre mountains of Mexico. Glaciers and other habitat barriers isolated populations and resulted in the variances we see in today's bighorns. In general terms we can divide North American wild sheep into two species, the thinhorns in the north, and bighorns in the south, with each of these being further divided into two distinct sub-species. In the northernmost parts of their range the white Dall's sheep sub-species dominates, giving way to the Stone's sheep variety in the Yukon and British Columbia

Texas' Desert Bighorns

The good news is that there are efforts to restore bighorns to places where they once lived. Desert bighorns disappeared from Texas in 1960. The Texas Bighorn Society is dedicated to restoring these sheep to their historical habitat in the state's deserts. Read more about the society's work at its Web site.

Access this Web site from http://www.myreportlinks.com

old migration paths. Successful controlled burns in Wyoming, Idaho, and South Dakota helped expand the range of the bighorns' habitat.

Sometimes, restoring bighorn habitats involves removing stray cattle. The grazing cattle compete with the bighorns for available food. Anza-Borrego Desert State Park in southern California is the habitat of about 180 bighorn sheep. Between 1987 and 1989, employees of the park removed 117 cattle from its land.

▷ Captive Breeding of Bighorns

The Bighorn Institute in Palm Desert, California, has carried on a captive-breeding program. A herd

It is up to us to make sure that the majestic bighorn, like this desert bighorn, does not disappear from the American West forever.

of bighorns is kept in the institute's pens in Palm Desert. When lambs are born there, they are not allowed to become too accustomed to humans. This way, when they are released back to the wild, they will not be inclined to wander into towns or other areas where they will be at risk. The Bighorn Institute released seventy-seven captive-raised bighorn sheep into the wild between 1985 and 2000.

Organizations such as the Bighorn Institute, the Society for the Conservation of Bighorn Sheep, the Foundation for North American Wild Sheep (FNAWS), as well as federal agencies such as the U.S. Forest Service, the Bureau of Land Management, and the U.S. Fish and Wildlife Service are working to promote the survival of bighorn sheep. Various programs and activities have met with success.

Scientists are learning more about bighorn sheep all the time. Two populations of bighorns are still endangered species, but there are reasons to believe that they will still be with us for a long time to come. If that happens, visitors to bighorn wilderness habitats in the future will have the opportunity to be thrilled at the sight of these mountain monarchs scampering along the high crags. In the fall, the air will still echo with the loud clash of the sheep's mighty horns.

In 1973, Congress took the farsighted step of creating the Endangered Species Act, widely regarded as the world's strongest and most effective wildlife conservation law. It set an ambitious goal: to reverse the alarming trend of human-caused extinction that threatened the ecosystems we all share.

Each book in this series explores the life of an endangered animal. The books tell how and why the animals have become endangered and explain the efforts being made to restore their populations.

The United States Fish and Wildlife Service and the National Marine Fisheries Service share responsibility for administration of the Endangered Species Act. Over time, animals are added to, reclassified in, or removed from the federal list of Endangered and Threatened Wildlife and Plants. At the time of publication, all the animals in this series were listed as endangered species. The most up-to-date list can be found at **http://www.fws.gov/endangered/wildlife.html**.

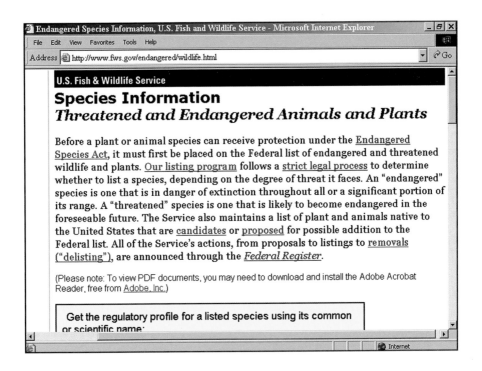

The Internet sites described below can be accessed at http://www.myreportlinks.com

▶**Rocky Mountain National Park: Bighorn Sheep**
Editor's Choice Read about the bighorn sheep brought back to Rocky Mountain National Park.

▶**Bighorn Institute**
Editor's Choice Learn about an organization dedicated to the conservation of bighorns.

▶**Mammal Fact Sheets: Mountain Sheep**
Editor's Choice This site offers text and video of Canada's mountain sheep.

▶**Colorado Division of Wildlife: Bighorn Sheep**
Editor's Choice At this Colorado wildlife division site, learn about that state's bighorn population.

▶**Sierra Nevada Bighorn Sheep Foundation**
Editor's Choice A foundation seeks to save the Sierra Nevada bighorn sheep.

▶**The Living Desert: Desert Bighorn**
Editor's Choice Find out more about desert bighorns and habitats from this zoo Web site.

▶**ADW: *Ovis canadensis***
A university site offers detailed information about bighorn sheep biology.

▶**Animal Field Guide: Bighorn Sheep**
This site presents a fact sheet about bighorns in Montana and contains excellent photographs.

▶**Bighorn Sheep in Hells Canyon**
The history and current restoration project to restore bighorns in Hells Canyon is described.

▶**Bighorn Sheep Relocated to Preserve Population**
Read a news release about the relocation of twenty-five Rocky Mountain bighorn sheep in 2005.

▶**Bighorn Sheep Threatened by Climate Change**
A university magazine article takes a look at how climate change is affecting desert bighorns.

▶**China Lake Petroglyphs**
Petroglyphs in the Coso Mountains indicate that native peoples were fascinated with bighorn sheep.

▶**Creativity Used to Medicate Bighorn Sheep**
Utah wildlife officials combine medicine with food to keep the state's bighorns parasite free.

▶**Creature Features: Desert Bighorn Sheep**
A museum site especially for children describes the characteristics of desert bighorn sheep.

▶**Desert and Rocky Mountain Bighorn Sheep Restored**
Arizona's bighorn population is boosted in 2006 thanks to wildlife biologists.

Report Links

The Internet sites described below can be accessed at
http://www.myreportlinks.com

▶**Desert Bighorn Council**
Learn about the release of thirty bighorns into the San Andres National Wildlife Refuge.

▶**Desert Bighorn Sheep of Cabeza Prieta NWR**
At this site, learn how desert bighorns in Arizona have adapted to life in a harsh environment.

▶**Foundation for North American Wild Sheep: For Kids**
Learn about the wild sheep of North America on this Web site.

▶**Inscription Canyon Rock Art Petroglyphs**
View petroglyphs of bighorn sheep made by the Paiute and Shoshone on canyon walls.

▶**Mammals: Goat and Sheep**
This San Diego Zoo site offers information about wild sheep, including bighorns.

▶*National Geographic:* **Rocky Mountain Bighorn Sheep**
This *National Geographic* Web site profiles Rocky Mountain bighorn sheep.

▶**NatureServe Explorer Bighorn Sheep**
Browse a database of information about bighorn sheep.

▶**Nature Works: Big Horn Sheep—*Ovis canadensis***
A public television site offers information on endangered bighorns.

▶**NPS Archeology Program: Coso Rock Art**
View bighorn sheep petroglyphs from the Coso Rock Art District.

▶**Sierra Nevada Bighorn Sheep: A Brief History**
Read about protection for a population of Sierra Nevada bighorns.

▶**Texas' Desert Bighorns**
The Texas Bighorn Society is working to restore Texas's wild sheep population.

▶**Thinhorn Sheep**
This site offers information about North America's other wild sheep, the thinhorn.

▶**USFWS Endangered Species Program Kid's Corner**
This USFWS Web site offers ways you can help save endangered species.

▶**Write Your Representative**
Find links to your congressional representatives on this government site.

▶**Yosemite National Park—Nature & Science**
Yosemite National Park is one of two national parks where Sierra Nevada bighorns live.

annular ring—A deep groove on a bighorn sheep's horn; annular rings tell a sheep's age.

Beringia—The land bridge that existed across the Bering Strait, connecting Siberia and Alaska during ice ages when the sea level dropped.

brooming—Wearing down of the tips of the horns.

browse—Leaves, shoots, and twigs of shrubs and other woody plants.

Continental Divide—A series of mountain ridges mostly along the Rocky Mountains that divide the North American continent's rivers into east-flowing and west-flowing bodies of water.

crag—A steep rock or cliff.

cud—Regurgitated food brought up into the mouth of a ruminant, such as a sheep, from its first stomach, or rumen, to be chewed again.

epizootic—An outbreak of disease among a population of animals.

ewes—Female sheep.

forbs—Herbs and other low-growing broadleaf plants.

guard hair—Long, coarse hair that protects an undercoat of hair on a mammal.

habitat—The place where an animal or a plant normally lives.

herbivore—An animal that eats plants.

home range—The area of land used by the members of a species throughout their lives.

keratin—A tough, fibrous protein material that forms the outer part of the horns of a bighorn sheep.

predators—Animals that hunt other animals for food.

prerut—The period before rutting or mating season, in which bighorn rams have fights to determine dominance.

rams—Male sheep.

rumen—The first chamber in the stomach of a ruminant.

ruminant—An animal with a multichambered stomach and a complex digestive system.

scabies—An infestation of mites in the ears.

species—A group of organisms so similar to one another that they can interbreed.

subspecies—A group within a species that refers to a population of a particular region that is different from other such populations of the same species and can still interbreed successfully with them.

thinhorns—One of two species of North American wild sheep; bighorns are the other. Thinhorns are mountain sheep that live in the northern latitudes.

transplantation—Moving a group, such as bighorns, to new areas.

Chapter 1. Kings of the Crags

1. Lisa Mighetto, ed., *Muir Among the Animals: The Wildlife Writings of John Muir* (San Francisco: Sierra Club Books, 1986), p. 6.

2. Ibid., p. 14.

3. U.S. Fish and Wildlife Service, *Endangered Species Bulletin,* March 2006.

4. *Sierra Nevada Bighorn Sheep Foundation,* "Overview," n.d., <http://www.sierrabighorn.org/Pages/S-Overview.htm> (October 13, 2006).

5. Clinton W. Epps, et al., "Bighorn Sheep Threatened by Climate Change," *Conservation Biology,* February 2004.

6. The Sierra Club, "Endangered Species Act," Petition, *Support a Strong Endangered Species Act,* n.d., <https://secure2.convio.net/sierra/site/Advocacy?cmd=display&page=UserAction&id=143> (November 14, 2006).

Chapter 2. Origin, Habitats, and Distribution of Bighorn Sheep

1. I. McT. Cowan, "Distribution and variation in the native sheep of North America," *American Midland Naturalist,* 24:505–580, 1940.

2. R.R. Ramey II, *Evolutionary Genetics and Systematics of North American Mountain Sheep,* Ph.D. Thesis, Cornell University, Ithaca, N.Y., 1993; and J.D. Wehausen and R.R. Ramey II, *A Morphometric Reevaluation of the Peninsular Bighorn Subspecies,* Trans. Desert Bighorn Council, 37:1–10, 1993.

3. Bert Gildart, *Mountain Monarchs: Bighorn Sheep* (Minnetonka, Minn.: NorthWord Press, 1999), p. 23.

4. Ibid., 102.

Chapter 3. Physical Characteristics of Bighorn Sheep

1. Lisa Mighetto, ed., *Muir Among the Animals: The Wildlife Writings of John Muir* (San Francisco: Sierra Club Books, 1986), p. 11.

2. Bert Gildart, *Mountain Monarchs: Bighorn Sheep* (Minnetonka, Minn.: NorthWord Press, 1999), p. 47.

3. Ibid.

4. Ibid., p. 37.

5. Ibid.

6. Ibid., p. 40.

7. United States Department of the Interior, National Park Service, *Fauna of the National Parks of the United States*, "The Bighorn of Death Valley," Ralph E. Welles and Florence B. Welles, Fauna Series No. 6, United States Government Printing Office, Washington, D.C., 1961, <http://www.cr.nps.gov/history/online_books/fauna6/fauna2c.htm> (February 20, 2007).

8. Brian M. Wikeem and Michael D. Pitt, "Grazing effects and range trend assessment on California bighorn sheep range," *Journal of Range Management,* vol. 44, number 5, September 1991, Abstract.

Chapter 4. Bighorn Behavior

1. Olaus J. Murie, *Animal Tracks* (Boston: Houghton Mifflin Company, 1982), p. 303.

2. Bert Gildart, *Mountain Monarchs: Bighorn Sheep* (Minnetonka, Minn.: NorthWord Press, 1999), p. 76.

Chapter 5. History of Bighorn-Human Contact

1. Bert Gildart, *Mountain Monarchs: Bighorn Sheep* (Minnetonka, Minn.: NorthWord Press, 1999), p. 117.

2. Dale E. Toweill and Valerius Geist, *Return of Royalty: Wild Sheep of North America* (Missoula, Mont.: Boone and Crockett Club and Foundation for North American Wild Sheep, 1999), p. 4.

3. Ibid., p. 5.

4. Ibid.

5. J.A. Allen, *Bulletin of the American Museum of Natural History,* "Article 1: Historical and Nomenclatorial Notes on North American Sheep," vol. XXXI, 1912, pp. 9–10 <http://digitallibrary.amnh.org/dspace/bitstream/2246/1793/1/B031a01.pdf> (November 27, 2006).

6. Toweill and Geist, p. 6.

7. Ibid.

8. Ibid.

9. Ibid., p. 7.

Chapter 6. Threats to the Sheep's Survival

1. William J. Foreyt, "Fatal *Pasteurella Haemolytica* Pneumonia in Bighorn Sheep After Direct Contact With Clinically Normal Domestic Sheep," *American Journal of Veterinary Research,* 1989, p. 341.

2. Francis J. Singer, Elizabeth Williams, Michael W. Miller, and Linda C. Zeigenfuss, "Population Growth, Fecundity, and Survivorship in Recovering Populations of Bighorn Sheep," *Restoration Ecology,* December 2000, p. 75.

Chapter 7. Current Efforts to Protect Bighorn Sheep

1. Mitch Tobin, "Lion Kill Would Aid Bighorns, State Says," *Arizona Daily Star,* July 18, 2001, p. A4.

2. Ibid.

Further Reading

Bannor, Brett. *Bighorn Sheep.* San Diego, Calif.: Lucent Books, 2003.

Bograd, Larry. *The Rocky Mountains.* New York: Benchmark Books, 2001.

Grupper, Jonathan. *Destination—Rocky Mountains.* Washington, D.C.: National Geographic Society, 2001.

Lasky, Kathryn. *John Muir: America's First Environmentalist.* Cambridge, Mass: Candlewick Press, 2006.

Mattern, Joanne. *Wildlife of North America: Bighorn Sheep.* Mankato, Minn: Capstone Press, 2006.

Muir, John. *The Mountains of California.* New York: The Modern Library, 2001.

Pfeffer, Wendy. *High Mountains.* New York: Benchmark Books, 2003.

Snedden, Robert. *Mountains.* North Mankato, Minn.: Smart Apple Media, 2005.

Stone, Tanya Lee. *Unique Animals of the Mountains and Prairies.* Detroit: Blackbirch Press, 2005.